The Next Level Dropshipping Guide

How to Elevate your Income and Create a Lucrative Long-term Business from Anywhere in the world with Facebook Advertising, Shopify, And Fulfillment Centers

Table of Contents

Introduction

Congratulations on downloading "The Next Level Dropshipping Guide: How to Elevate your Income and Create a Lucrative Long-term Business from Anywhere in the world with Facebook advertising, Shopify, And Fulfillment Centers."

The chapters highlighted in this guide will discuss everything that you need to know in order to start off with your own dropshipping business. There are a lot of different types of businesses that you can choose to work with. Many of them claim to be part-time and can offer you a lot of money on the side, but most of them end up failing, taking up too much time, and not providing you with the money that was promised.

Dropshipping is a process that is different from these other options. With this method, you get the benefit of working the hours that are best for you. If you want just to work a few hours a week, you simply have to just sell a few products at a time to keep the time management easy. If you want to turn this into a full-time income source, you simply scale the business up and start selling more products and advertising more. There really isn't any other business model that works as successfully as working with dropshipping.

This guidebook is going to take some time to look at all the information that you need to know to kick off with dropshipping. We will take a look at what dropshipping is, some of the advantages of working with dropshipping, how to choose a good supplier and a good product to work with, and more to get things started.

Inside, we will also have a discussion about which platforms are the best for helping you to see results with your selling. You can choose to create your personal website and sell the products through that method, or you can work through some other popular websites such as Shopify, Amazon, or eBay to sell your products.

In addition, we will spend time looking at all the other parts of dropshipping that are important to get the most out of this business and get it to work for you. We will look at how to keep your website safe so customers trust you with their payments, how to work with social media to grow your website, how to provide the best customer service each time, and even some methods on how you can beat out the competition and get ahead.

While there are many other business opportunities out there that you can choose to work with, none are going to be as successful and as easy to start as dropshipping. While you will need to put in a little bit of work to get this started, you will find that compared to some of the other methods of making money from home, this is one of the best. As soon as you are ready to kick off with your own dropshipping business, make sure to read through this guidebook to learn how!

Chapter 1: Specialization

Dropshipping is a fairly new branch of e-commerce where entrepreneurs buy and sell goods directly to the customers without having to put up huge amounts of capital and without having to hold onto large amounts of inventory. Most people who hear about dropshipping for the first time find the notion a bit confusing, but in actual sense, it's pretty simple to grasp.

If you are in this business, all you have to do is find people who are willing to buy certain goods, find suppliers who are selling those goods, purchase the goods from the suppliers at a lower price, sell it to the buyers at a higher price, then pocket the difference. What's more, you can ship the product directly from your suppliers to your customers, so you don't have to hold onto inventory at any given time.

The concept itself is that simple—the execution, however, is much more complicated.

The main difference between traditional retail practice and dropshipping is that you as an entrepreneur or a merchant don't have to stock up or even own stock at any point in time. All you have to do is buy as much inventory as you need and exactly when you need it from someone else who sells in bulk. Once you have received an order from a customer, you can buy from a wholesaler or even directly from the manufacturer of the item for the purpose of fulfilling that order. This model allows you to stay liquid at all times because you don't ever have to invest your money on the stock. You just have to wait until you have received a payment from a customer, and then pay a certain fraction of that payment to the supplier to cover the item and shipping costs.

In e-commerce textbooks, dropshipping is referred to as a "supply chain management method," and it can be used in both online and brick and mortar stores, but the concept has become more popular with the rise of e-commerce because it's much more viable as a model for online stores. Just like in ordinary retail businesses, the profit margin that you have to work with as a drop-shipper is the difference between the wholesale price and the retail price of the product that you are selling.

1

1 [1] https://www.shopify.com/guides/dropshipping/understanding-dropshipping

How the Dropshipping Model Operates

To start a dropshipping business, the very first step you should consider is to find an item that you intend to sell. This first part is really challenging because there are already thousands of other dropshipping companies online that are already in operation, so you can't just wake up one day and start selling a certain product—you may find it hard to outdo the person who has already developed trust with customers. All you should do is select a niche and think of ways to be unique from other business persons.

Finding the right niche for your dropshipping business isn't easy—it requires you to do a lot of research. You must identify the area where you can fill a market gap, where you can create added value (either by providing products that are slightly better or by providing valuable information to go along with those products), where you can provide products that are difficult to find locally, or where you can provide products that are slightly more affordable than those of your competitors.

After you have a niche, the next step is to find a supplier for your product(s). There are specific characteristics of a good supplier that you will have to look out for. First, the supplier has to be one who is willing to drop-ship. There are some suppliers who may frown upon the idea of having to release their products through you as a middle-man, so you should find out early enough if they work with drop-shippers to avoid wasting your time on them. Other wholesale suppliers may be unwilling to break their large batches of products to send out orders one by one. You need to evaluate your ideas thoroughly to get a supplier who has the capacity to fulfill all your customers' orders and one whose business model is optimized for dropshipping.

Next, you have to correspond with your suppliers to make sure that they meet your requirements in relation to shipping methods, shipping times, quality control, prices, etc. For your dropshipping business to work, your supplier must be completely reliable, and the relationship between you two must be built on solid ground. Most wholesalers who work with dropshipping businesses keep a roster which you will have to join. For you to join a wholesaler's or supplier's roster, you have to provide details about your business, and in many cases, you may have to pay a membership fee.

You have to identify specific products that you will be selling and make sure that your supplier has a sizable stock of that product, and then you have to set up an account with that supplier. You may notice that there are several variations of a particular product, but there are specific variations that do particularly well in the market. Even if you have already decided on a niche, you should take time to do a bit of market research before you pick specific makes and models of the product.

Setting up an account with a supplier may require you to provide some documentation to prove that you are a valid business enterprise, and you may have to sign some documents that are provided by the supplier. The supplier might want to see applicable business licenses from you, and the two of you may have to come to an agreement on terms such as payment rates, methods, and schedules. You may have to sign a binding contract in some instances.

Dropshipping businesses are enterprises like any others, so they have to be structured as legally-recognizable entities. You may have to register your dropshipping business as a company, a proprietorship, or a corporation, depending on your own personal preferences and on the volume of business that you opt to transact through it. If the law requires your dropshipping company to have certain licenses, ensure that you acquire them. Dropshipping businesses also need to be registered for federal tax—you may use your own social security number for tax purposes if you have a proprietorship, but you have to get a tax ID if you have used other legal structures for the business.

Dropshipping businesses are either run on specific e-commerce platforms or on standalone e-commerce websites. Should you be yearning to start a dropshipping business, you have to choose between selling your products in an existing marketplace and actually creating your own online store.

If you choose to sell your products in a marketplace that already exists, you may run a possibility of being overshadowed by multiple other sellers who have products that are similar to yours. If you choose to set up your own e-commerce shop, you can use a service that helps you create your shop, or you can opt to set up your online shop after you purchase your own domain name from the starting point. However, every action taken comes with its own issues though the best choice for you would be to diversify. It's better to get listed in multiple platforms and marketplaces just to reach the largest possible pool of customers.

Should you opt for coming up with your own website for the purpose of dropshipping business, it is advisable to find a secure and reliable hosting service and a great domain name for your business. In the case that you have decent web design skills, put them to use and create a unique and captivating website. If you can't do web design, hire a trustworthy professional designer to do it for you. You will require a merchant account which is built into your website along with a shopping cart to give you an opportunity to make sells. Should you be selling on a marketplace that already exists (e.g., Amazon, eBay, etc.), you will have to create an account titled "seller."

Dropshipping businesses need to set up the necessary digital infrastructure to accept payments, so as you list yourself in various marketplaces, or while you come up with your own e-commerce website, set up a system where you can receive payments by credit card, PayPal, or any other ways. You may also have to provide your customers with a toll-free number where they can call you or any other means through which they can get in touch with you such as an email address in case they have any problems with your product.

Listing products on your page in an online marketplace or on your site isn't that complicated. Most suppliers and wholesalers make it easy for drop-shippers to just copy and paste pictures of the products that they want to sell. Wholesalers also provide detailed descriptions of their products which you can copy-paste, modify, and post on your site together with the photos. To be different from other retailers, you will have to think of your own unique content for the description on your site instead of just copying whatever the wholesaler provides.

For your dropshipping business to work, it is vital to have your pricing just right. If you choose to price your products too low, you may not be in a position to generate enough of a profit to make your efforts worthwhile. Should you set your charges too high, you may not effectively compete with other retailers who are selling similar products at a more affordable price. To set the right price, consider what you are paying the supplier, what the supplier is charging you for shipping, and what percentage of profit you intend to make. Should you bump into a rare product that is on high demand, you may make high percentages of profits. However, with most products, your best option will be to keep your prices close or similar to wholesaler's recommended retail price. That's because most other retailers will do the same, and you will be at a disadvantage if you tried to price your products differently.

The dropshipping model may also work for auction sites (e.g., eBay). You can list your products as new, set a minimum price for the product, and start your bidding countdown clock. If you are using an auction website to sell your dropshipping products, ensure that at the very least, the minimum bid should cover the cost of the product plus shipping to avoid making losses. The remaining process is the same as it is for non-auction sites—you have to send the product directly from the supplier to the winner's address after the payment has already been made.

Until a shipping point arises, a dropshipping business should have clear shipping and return policies that customers are made to understand from the very beginning. Should you want to set up your business in an existing marketplace, make sure that you understand and comply with any of the shipping rules of that marketplace and make sure that you convey the same rules to your buyers.

After everything is set up, the next step to concentrate on is to market your store and wait for someone to purchase your products. There are lots of online marketing techniques which you can deploy. You should create a mailing list of all your customers so that you may be drum up some repeat business from them. You can send out updates about new products, promotions, and other offers. You can consider social media marketing techniques, blogs, online videos, and other internet marketing methods to bring in customers. Driving traffic to your sales page isn't easy, but it's a skill that anyone can perfect with determination and hard work. You can also offer special sales, contests, and other promotions to pique the interest of potential customers and to increase your sales.

The moment a customer makes a purchase, you need to act immediately by turning around and ordering that exact same product from your wholesaler. The minute you verify that the customer has paid for his or her order, you should go ahead and relay the product to the supplier. Try to avoid delays at all costs, because the last thing you want is to fail to deliver to your customer on time.

As for saving time, you should have a notification system in place just to ensure that you know about order placements when they happen. If you can afford to, hire one or more people to act on customer orders in real time. Pay the supplier, and instruct him to ship the product to the customer's address. If the supplier provides you with a tracking number for your shipment, use it to monitor the shipment and ensure that everything is on schedule.

The customers also need to know about the progress of their shipments, so set up a mechanism where they can be automatically notified once the shipment is sent out. After you have closed the sale, send them subsequent emails telling them when their products would be shipped and the time they can expect to receive them. Be available to receive calls and to address their concerns in case any problems arise.

For the dropshipping business to work, it is vital that you have open lines of getting in touch with your suppliers so that you can find solutions to issues as soon as possible. The shipping process has many inherent risks—products may break during transit, and you may need to replace them in the shortest time possible. In other cases, you may experience problems with your supplier—he may either fail to send out your product on time, or he may run out of stock.

As a retailer, your reputation depends on your ability to deliver on your shipment on time. The problem of back ordering occurs rather frequently with some suppliers, especially those who service multiple retailers. Should your supplier run short of stock, you may be unable to fulfill a customer's order, and you may be forced to cancel on him, which could reflect poorly on you if the customers chose to complain about your service delivery online or to give you a negative rating or review.

You have to take measures to prevent a case where you are forced to cancel orders because your supplier is out of stock. It may be in your best interest to build some redundancy into your system by having more than one supplier so that if the main one is unable to deliver for any reason, you may order your product from your backup supplier.

As a dropshipping retailer, it's absolutely crucial that you keep the fact that you are sourcing your product somewhere else hidden from both your current and your prospective customers. The survival of your business relies on people believing that you are the best source of whatever product they are looking for. If they discover that you are sourcing your product from a third party and selling it to them, they may opt to cut you out of the whole process and try to buy the product from the supplier by themselves.

To conceal your suppliers from your customers, you have to practice what is known as "blind shipping." Blind shipping is a process where you ship your products without including a return address on the package or a receipt from the supplier. Remember that in dropshipping, the product goes directly from your supplier to your customer. If the supplier puts a receipt inside the package, the customer will notice that the supplier's name is different from your business name, and he may decide to Google the supplier and order from him the next time he wants something.

A common alternative to "blind shipping" is called "private-label shipping." It involves shipping a product directly from the supplier to the customer, but instead of listing the supplier's address as the return address, a customized slip from the retailer is stuck onto the package. The customized slip would contain the retailer's logo and contact information so that if the customer had a problem with his shipment, he would contact the retailer and ask for a way forward rather than sending the package back. Most major suppliers who work with dropshipping retailers will allow you to create a customized package slip if you choose to practice "private-label shipping."

For your dropshipping business to work correctly, the final thing that you have to is to follow up on your customers to ensure they are satisfied after their purchase orders have been delivered. If customers have any complaints that are specific to your product (e.g., its quality, how it's packaged, or how it's delivered), it is your responsibility to address those concerns to their satisfaction and then learn from them to improve your services. At the end of the day, dropshipping works best if there exists a personal touch to your service delivery.

At face value, dropshipping may seem like an easy process that anyone can wake up one day and start doing, but that's not the reality. For you to succeed in this business, it is a must to be deliberate, dedicated, and determined. Like any other low-risk business, dropshipping has attracted many entrepreneurs, and because of the resulting competition, the business has become less lucrative and harder to break into than it was some time back. That doesn't mean that it's no longer a viable business model. It just means that if you want to excel, you need to be more pragmatic in your approach to the business.

Don't go into dropshipping with unrealistic expectations of making supernormal profits overnight. Instead, you should take your time to study the market and to identify products whose profitability can be predicted with a level of surety. Your decision to market and sell a certain product shouldn't be based on hype. Instead, it should be based on the analysis of market data, which can clearly tell you if there is an existing market for that product.

2

---

2 [2] https://mywifequitherjob.com/why-dropshipping-isnt-as-easy-and-simple-as-you-think/

Chapter 2: Benefits and some downfalls in dropshipping

The Benefits of Working in Dropshipping

There exist many distinct business opportunities out there that you can select to go with. However, none of them provide the same benefits that you can acquire from starting your own dropshipping business. This type of business does not necessarily need a lot of money to start, can take just a few steps to get it up and running, introduces you to a global market right from the start, and so much more. Let's highlight some of the benefits of working with your own dropshipping business and why you should consider starting yours today.

Little Investment to Start

Starting your own dropshipping business requires very little investment to get going. You don't have to pay to come up with the products, you don't have to keep an inventory for the products, and you do not have to employ a team to help you run the business or even to pay for shipping. In fact, it is possible to get started with drop shipping without paying for anything upfront.

If you choose to sell the products from your own website, although there are some benefits attached to it, you will have to pay a bit to get the website up and running. In the case that you choose to go with Amazon or eBay, you can get the item listed and then afterward, you will pay once the item actually sells. If you plan to consider a bit for advertising to draw more interest to your items, then you will need to reimburse for that too.

When operating in a dropshipper position, it is really in your control how much you hope to pay out to kick off. Some people are able to start this kind of business for nothing, and others like to spend a bit to help set themselves apart from other sellers. Something amazing about this business is that you get to be the one who decides all of it, and you can keep the costs as low as you need.

Easy to start off

While we will discuss this in a bit more detail later, it is pretty easy to start off with your own dropshipping business. Unlike some other business models, you will notice that this business can be started relatively quickly. Keep in mind that you do need to do a bit of research on suppliers and products. It is vital not to rush in and pick the first product you see. But comparatively, you can't find an easier type of business.

With dropshipping, you simply need to find a niche to work in, find a product and the right supplier of that product to fill that niche, list it in some manner online (such as on Amazon or your own website), and then wait for a customer order. Once the customer orders, you will take what they pay you and place an order directly with the suppliers. The supplier will then send the item out to the customer, and you will end up with a happy customer.

Of course, there will always be moments when things won't move as exactly as you had planned, but there are strategies you can implement to minimize issues and keep things going smoothly. Those basic steps above are really all you need to begin with this kind of business model.

Little to No Overhead Costs

As a dropshipper, you will have limited to no overhead costs. You are not required to keep any of the products on hand or to have an inventory of any kind at all. With this business model, you simply list the products that you intend to sell somewhere online such as on Amazon or eBay. Then, when a customer orders, you will use that money to place an order directly with the supplier. After that, the supplier ships the item straight to the customer, not to you. You do not need to be worried when it comes to having all of the products on hand for each customer, which means there is very little cost for you.

There are some costs that come with dropshipping, but you do have some control over them. For example, should you use your own website, you may have to include a bit of money into that. There is an attached fee for listing on eBay and Amazon as well. If you wish to advertise on social media, you will also need to pay a little bit. However, as a business proprietor, you can choose the amount of cash you intend to spend on the products. And despite the other expenses, there will never be an overhead cost for running your business.

Lots of Products to Choose From

In dropshipping business, you will find that there are a ton of products to choose from to sell later for your business. There are hundreds of suppliers, and each of them can offer you something unique to work with. This means that it is easier for you to reach your own niche because there is sure to be a product out there that will work for you.

Make sure that you take the time to really look through a

bunch of suppliers and the products that they offer. It is crucial to make sure that you find a good supplier, a unique product, and something that is in high demand but is still not getting reached well by other sellers. The moment you combine all of these together, then be sure to find a product that will attract more sales on your site.

A Global Market

Since dropshipping and the entire business you do with it will occur online, you get the opportunity to work with a global market, even as a beginner. With a traditional business, you will have to start out by working in your local community. After some time has passed and you see a good amount of profits and interest, you may decide to expand out into your area, then the state, and later on the country. Eventually, you may decide to reach out to a global market, but that is only if your business gets that far. Many businesses are happy to just expand a little bit in their region.

But with dropshipping, you can make your products available to a large market right from the beginning. If you list on sites like eBay, Amazon, and Shopify, or in case you do your own website, you are already reaching a potential global market. This is huge. That means more people who may potentially be interested in your product and more potential to grow your own dropshipping business in no time.

Easy to Scale Later on If You Want

When you first get started with this kind of business, you hope to simplify everything in it. You may only want to start out with a few products to keep it simple and learn the ropes, and that is just fine. But over time, as you start to get the hang of dropshipping and everything that goes along with it. You can then decide to scale your business and make it bigger later on.

That is part of the beauty of working with this kind of field. It is upon you to make it as small or as big as you would like. Some people keep it smaller with just a few products for sale. Others decide to grow this into a large business with hundreds of items that they look forward to selling. And scaling it in this manner is very easy. You simply do a bit of research and decide what other products you would like to sell on your chosen sites, and then you list them.

Easy to Automate

At the very starting point, it will be ideal to give out more of your time and effort into your business. This is necessary to get any business up and running properly. It is advisable to find good suppliers, pick out the right products to sell, get things listed, and so on. This takes up some time and can result in a lot of people giving up with dropshipping early on.

But if you are able to get through the beginning work with dropshipping and you are able to be successful with growing your business, you will find that you are in a position to modify your field and make it more automated. This can really help to save you a lot of your time and hassle. You can get your social media posts to be automated, you can handle the orders and any emails within a few hours at any time of the day that you choose, and most of the business will run itself.

Think of how it will feel to make unlimited money with a side business where most of the work is automated! This is what most people dream about when they get started with dropshipping in the first place. You have to go through and put in the hard work from the beginning, but if you can do that, you will soon be able to automate the whole business, and this can really help things to grow.

There are lots of advantages associated with beginning your

own dropshipping business. You can reach a global market. It doesn't cost a lot to get started. You don't have to keep inventory or worry about the overhead costs, and so much more. As for anyone yearning to put in the hard work to make a good income, dropshipping is the way to go.

3

3 [3] https://multichannelmerchant.com/blog/7-business-advantages-drop-shipping/

The limitations of Dropshipping

Dropshipping business has a lot of privileges that you can love. It is a great way to start earning an income on the side along with your regular line of work. Be sure to enjoy a variety of products to sell, you can choose how much or how little you would like to sell, and you get the freedom of choosing times to work that goes around your busy schedule. Having said all that, there are some downsides that when you decide to get into the dropshipping business, which is why only a few people have seen success with this business model. Some of the main drawbacks that you may notice with dropshipping include:

Sudden Shortages in Stock

As a dropshipper, it is your responsibility to keep up with the quantity of stock that is available from your supplier. You can then keep this information updated on your shop so that customers know when an item is out of stock or not. Sometimes, this is easy to do. But around the holidays, or with a really popular item, it is hard to keep up with the numbers.

Should there arise a sudden shortage in the stock of an item, this can pose a problem for you. Your customers may get frustrated that they can't get ahold of that item right away. And if the customer already placed an order for that item, and then you found out that item was out of stock, this can really make it difficult for you and the buyer.

The best way to handle this is to have multiple suppliers for the same item or at least two or three suppliers with similar items. This way, if your main supplier ends up running out of a particular item, and you have customers interested, you still have some options. If the items are the same, you just switch suppliers for a moment and send the item out. If the items are a bit different, you can contact the customer and give them the alternative.

Customer Service is All on You

When the customer gets upset about something, they are not going to call up or email the supplier. You are the face of the business. And for all they know, you are completely in control of that product. When things go wrong, it is up to you to handle all of the customer service yourself.

This can get tedious and hard on some occasions. It is your duty to handle any questions that the customer has. Also, it is your responsibility to answer emails when you get comments or questions or complaints from a customer. If there need to be any returns or exchanges, you are the one who will have to handle all of this. As one person, this can seem like a lot and can really add to the workload in some situations.

Less Control Over Your Own Business

Dropshipping is a great business to get into. You can start to earn money on products that other companies make, and you don't have to keep any inventory on hand or actually make the product yourself. But, the tradeoff here is that you possess very little control over your own business. The suppliers you pick will be the ones in most control over this kind of business. And if you pick the wrong supplier, it could mean the end of your business.

As a dropshipper, you are basically listing items for sale online for other companies. You list them for higher than the supplier has them, and then you take the profits. You will have a customer place the order through you, and then you take that money and place the request via the supplier. From there, the supplier takes over.

If you have picked out good suppliers to operate along with, this procedure should be easy to handle. After placing your order, they will make the product, ship it out, and your customer will be happy. But you have very little control over this. It is possible that the supplier could send the product to the wrong place, orders can get mixed up, and more. And when these happen, you have to handle the downfall, even though you didn't have control over any of it.

Potential Issues with Quality Control

Since you are not the one making the product and you never actually touch the product, there could be issues with product quality. The supplier will often try to do the best they can because that is how they make money as well. But if there are quality control issues, you are the one who is going to get harmed the most. Your customers will leave bad reviews, and there is no much you can do since you don't make the product.

There are some techniques you can use to ascertain that you provide high-quality products to your customers. First, when you are looking for a supplier, do some research on them. Look around and see what other dropshippers have thought about the products. Analyze and evaluate if there are any major problems with that company that you should be worried about. If there are many negative reviews or other issues, choose to go with someone else.

Before you decide whether you are going to sell a particular product or not, consider ordering one for yourself. This way, you can notice a good feeling for the experience the customer will have if they order through you. You can check how the shipping is, check in with the customer service, and see how the product actually works when you have it in your hand. Do this any time you decide to operate along with a new supplier for your business.

Hard to Find Products That Will Make Enough Money

One challenge that a good number of dropshippers will run into is finding a product they can make a good profit margin on. There are tons of companies and suppliers who will work with this kind of business model. Nonetheless, you need to be certain that you choose a product that is worth your time to sell. If you look at the price from the supplier and the product is listed as $10, but everyone online is charging $10.50, then this is probably not a good product for you to sell because you will have to sell quite a few to make anything for your time.

Many companies are like this, which is why dropshipping sometimes gets a bad name. It is important to take your time and not rush into the product that you want to work with. The higher the margin, the easier it is for you to make a good deal of profit on it, and the more worth your time it is.

Don't waste your time making just $0.50 on each item that you sell. By the time you put in the work, do your social media, and pay the fees for the listing site, you will end up losing money. Find products that make as much as possible. For example, if you can find a product that costs $50 from the supplier, but other similar sellers have it listed online at $200, then this is actually a product you should look into.

Supplier Errors

There are times when the supplier may make an error in one of the orders that you place. They may get an address mixed up and send the product to the wrong place. They may send the wrong product to one of your customers. Or they could make some other mistake that makes the customer upset.

When you are a dropshipper, it is hard to get the supplier to take on the hassle with this one. However, there are other good ones that will help out with this, but the customer is still going to be mad at you if something goes wrong with one of the orders. If this happens too often, you could run into the issue of too many mistakes and bad reviews, and then no customer will want to purchase from you in the future.

It is best to find a supplier you can trust. One that is known for getting orders right and for great customer satisfaction. Remember that you are the face of the business. If you sell the product, then the customer is going to blame you for things going wrong. Even though you are only listing the product and placing the order, the customer will assume you are the one in control of everything and will take their disappointment and frustration out on you. Picking out a good supplier who takes care of their customers can lead to a world of distinction when it comes to how successful you will become.

While there are many benefits to choosing dropshipping as your new business, there are also some aspects that you should put into thoughtfulness before starting. There is some extra activity that comes with this kind of business. And even though the income potential can be high, you do have to put in more effort and time to find a good supplier, someone who has great customer satisfaction, creates a high-quality product, and who will get the orders to the right people each time. In the case that you are able to do that, you can easily avoid some negative aspects that come with dropshipping.

4

---

4 [4] https://www.apsfulfillment.com/shipping-fulfillment/what-are-the-disadvantages-of-drop-shipping/

Chapter 3: Branding

Branding of your business will require some steps. Let's analyze all the steps involved.

Choosing a Niche

The very first idea you should think of is selecting a niche. This is essentially a category of products and/or a demographic. The emphasis on a niche is really about minimizing the size of your competition. If you wanted to be an online Walmart, then you have to compete with Walmart. However, if you want to sell specialty kitchen items, your competition dramatically drops. If you want to sell discount jewelry, it means you need to work along with your fellow jewelry sellers. The more defined a niche, assuming there's a large enough market to support it, the easier it is to make a profit and work your way up to a top spot in the industry. This is especially true when search engine discovery is one of your major methods of marketing.

So, how do we choose a niche that is appropriate for sales? We have several methods, so let's discuss them.

Something You Love?

The most obvious place people tend to start is to consider what types of products they love. It is not wise to blindly work in a niche just for this reason. There are no guarantees that your interests will be viable niches to market as an e-commerce site that works via dropshipping. However, that doesn't mean it's not worth taking the time to research these things.

Start making your list of potential niches by writing down the types of products you love. If you're obsessed with yo-yos, that may not be a great niche to center a store around, but if you love extreme sports, there are a huge amount of products you might market in that niche.

After this, you will need to consider what other people love.

Research Niche Criteria

When trying to determine if a niche is viable, there are some easy criteria you should consider. Taking these criteria into account will greatly simplify the process of determining if a niche is going to work well for you.

i.   Competition

How large is the competition for each niche you're considering? Are there huge stores that dominate the marketplace? The easiest way to begin gauging the competition is simply typing the most obvious keywords into Google. If you're interested in selling kids' clothes, you would type in "kids' clothes" and then potentially a second search for "kids' clothing store." When reviewing the results, it is ideal to take time looking at the "Shopping" results as well, which will pull up specific products and offer some insight into the stores that sell these items. If there is an overwhelming amount of sellers, then it may not be an ideal niche to work in. Your competition may be too large.

If you are unsure, the next step is to take a look at the Google Keyword Planner. This will require an Adwords account, but you do not have to start a campaign or pay anything before searching. Once you're logged in, you'll be able to type in keywords.

This will not only give you a highlight of related keywords, but it will tell you a few things about what people are searching for. Among the information will be a "monthly searches" number. This tells you how popular the search term (and, therefore, the niche) truly is.

From there, the next step is to look at how much it might cost to begin an ad campaign for any of these search terms. The more people are spending on advertisements, the more competition you truly have. If results show higher amounts of monthly searches and lower amounts of people spending money on advertising, it means that you have a better shot at being competitive in this niche.

ii.   Pricing

When choosing a niche, it is wise to consider the average prices of products within this niche. While having some lower-priced items is all right simply for add-on products, it is truly advised to focus on products over $100 and typically less than $1,000. Again, it's all right to have some higher-end items, but it shouldn't be the focus. If your desired niche simply doesn't have enough items within this price range, it is probably not worth pursuing.

There are a few reasons for this. First, there's really no profits to be made on low-priced items. Additionally, most low-priced products are not available for dropshipping because there's just not enough money in it for the supplier. With more expensive products, customer service becomes a headache. People spending over a certain amount are far more likely to ask for support, especially with technology, even if they simply don't know how to use it correctly. So, if your potential niche is mostly low-priced items or very high-priced items, it may not be a viable choice.

iii.   Weight

Heavier products are going to cost more for your supplier to ship, eating away at your profits. Smaller products are great because this isn't a huge concern. Though this may not be of concern to do away with a niche having heavy items, it is a major consideration, especially if you'd like to consider a global market.

iv.   Availability

Are the products simple to purchase locally? If they are, it may serve no great purpose to start an online store for this item. This is true because of many products even within niches that may be viable, but if the entire niche is something that's common in every city, it is wise to avoid it.

v.   Brands

The best niches will usually have products produced by many brands, and many of these brands will have high search volumes (check Google Keyword Planner) as well. Those niches where only a few brands are on the market are not going to be ideal because there's most likely little interest in the niche, or there's a brand that has the product patented, and you will have a difficult time diversifying with your products over time, making scalability suffer along the way.

When Several Pass the Criteria

If you narrow down your potential niches based on which pass these five criteria, it should become much simpler to choose a niche that actually suits your goals. If you're having a difficult time narrowing it down further, there are a few more things you might consider.

Can You Write About It?

Most great e-commerce startups will involve a large amount of writing. If you have several niches that feel viable, think which of these types of products would be the easiest for you to write a lot of quality content about. Taking this into consideration will save you from opening a store that you absolutely can't stand working on.

Can It Be Expanded?

Once you're successful, will you be able to expand the niche further? For example, if you open a skateboarding e-commerce store, you could later expand it into other extreme sports. If there's no room for growth, it may be less viable than another niche that is expandable. This isn't a rule of thumb, per se, but it is a consideration.

Is It "Evergreen?"

Do you have cause to trust that the product and niche will continue to thrive in years to come? If you're opening a fidget spinner store and then the trend dies off suddenly, you'll see a few months of profit followed by next to nothing. Finding products and niches that are "evergreen" and will continue to sell well into the future is a much better idea than jumping on something that's simply trending.

Additional Market/Product Research

If you're unsure, you can always take the time to conduct more market and product research on several niches. This is the most critical phase in the whole progress anyway, so, while it will take more time to research for several niches, it will give you the best overall image of what you're about to get yourself into!

Once You Choose a Niche

There's no telling if your niche is going to work out for you, but taking the time to make sure it meets certain criteria helps to take a lot of the risk out of the process. Now that you've started to minimize the risk by obtaining a strong idea of how well the market for your niche works, it is time to begin with the market research and product research that is going to help you develop a store that really works for you. This is important for many reasons, but largely because once you have a store, you'll need to understand your market in order to advertise to the appropriate crowds.

5

---

[5] https://www.dropshiplifestyle.com/profitable-niche-selection-explained/

Product description ideas

Now that you have a niche, a supplier, and a list of products you plan to sell in your store, it's almost time to put in the work involved in listing these products for sale. It is my suggestion to begin by writing the product description. This process is extremely important, and not taking it seriously is one of the biggest mistakes people make when approaching e-commerce for the first time.

The fact is that content is everything. This is true for many reasons. Not only does unique content that takes keyword research into consideration help with making your e-commerce store visible on search engines, but a compelling piece of copy can honestly create a customer out of someone that was previously just looking for a solution to their needs or wants. Let's discuss the many facets of the product description.

Don't Copy and Paste

While many dropshippers will claim that you can simply copy and paste product descriptions and images all day long into a store, the truth of the matter is that this can hurt your visibility on search engines. Likewise, as we've discussed briefly, most suppliers aren't in the business of selling to individual customers at retail.

The descriptions that they've written aren't aimed at consumers, and they most likely aren't compelling enough on their own. So, don't copy and paste. If you don't order the item and must use the manufacturer or supplier images, then this will get the job done, but any written content should definitely be written even if it is essentially the same in substance. If you do use the method of rewriting product descriptions, you can use plagiarism-checking services.

Keyword Integration

Taking the time to learn which keywords are most often searched and have the lowest amount of competition will help increase your search engine optimization and make your website more visible.

When integrating keywords into a product description, it's important to remember that everything should remain "organic." By "organic," I mean that it should come across as natural in your writing. It used to work to simply dump awkward key phrases into an article, but Google has long since changed its algorithm to avoid websites that spam their keywords like this. Likewise, it will turn off potential buyers and make your store seem less legitimate.

You should really only be using keywords a few times in any given product description or blog post. The rule has been to use a keyword only one time per 100 words. If it's natural to consider the word more, then it may be unavoidable, but if it doesn't need repeating, it is often best to minimize the number of times you integrate a keyword to only a few times per 500 words.

When integrating keywords, the best places to integrate them are into headings and titles. Google's bots specifically target headings because these are meant to indicate an extended amount of information related to the words within the heading. Naturally, the product title shouldn't have a keyword stuffed in it if it doesn't make sense to include it, but if it does make sense to include it, that's a huge bonus.

Headings

On the topic of headings, it is wise to use at least a few of these throughout your product description, especially if the description is a bit on the longer side. Headings help to break up content in an easy to digest manner, and if a customer if researching socks that help protect against clammy toes, then a heading that says, "Moisture Block Technology," may exactly be what you need to have them stop for a moment and actually read your (honest) sales pitch.

Bullet Points and Numbered Lists

It will be a cool idea to put list formats into use when possible. Many consumers aren't interested in reading every last word, and using bullet points to list off features at the beginning of a product description is an easy way to help them determine in the case they want to gain more knowledge about the product. Bullet points and numbered lists can also be used to explain exactly what comes with a kit or package as well.

Write For Your Niche

This particular skill may need to be developed if your niche isn't part of a community that you've been involved in for some time. One major way to increase sales is to understand your market as thoroughly as possible, write your content specifically towards them, and use your product description to offer solutions to their problems. Writing dry copy may work for some niches, but other niches may be heavily influenced by copywriting that specifically speaks to them.

More of this has to do with your personality or your ability to relate to others. The only solution is to become part of the communities that your target customer enjoys, talk with them regularly, and hopefully enjoy yourself. The other solution is to write the basic content and find someone that understands or belongs to the target market and hire them to edit the content for you (or have them write it entirely).

Benefits

When writing a product description, the overwhelming point is to show that there exist many benefits to buying a product. The ideal situation is that this is genuine, and that's part of the reason I suggest avoiding poor products during the selection process. The better the item, the easier it is to remind them with every sentence that this product is beneficial to them.

This is where the question, "How can I add value?" truly comes into play. What benefits to this product are you able to see that many (if not all) of your competitors have failed to highlight? What perspective is going to make us excited about the item?

Images

You absolutely should provide images of the products you are selling. It is advisable to have a fancy DSLR camera and that you personally purchase and test every item you list in your shop. Because that may not be practical for all of us, it may come down to using the pictures provided on the suppliers' websites. The more pictures, the better, and if you can get unique shots, then that is a huge plus.

Video

Again, this one requires that you have actually purchased the item. If you have purchased the item and have a decent camera and microphone, taking the time to review it on video is a great way to help push the sales. Video content can dramatically increase your sales. In the case that you cannot produce video yourself, it may be wise to link to some YouTube videos of others reviewing the products. However, be certain that you're not breaking any laws by sharing those, though.

Offer Other Items

One tip that's often left ignored by e-commerce entrepreneurs writing their own content is to also take the time to offer other products at the end of the description or at the bottom of the product page. I've offered a solution for this on Shopify in Chapter 11. When it makes sense to include accessories for the item at the bottom, take a few minutes to produce a list of popular items bought along with the product. For example, if you're selling a microphone, it may be wise to also suggest a microphone stand that's appropriate for the microphone. If things go your way, you could potentially make two sales instead of one.

Likewise, you can also offer comparable products in place of this particular item. Take your cue from Amazon here. Almost every product page will have an "other customers bought" section, and many of them will even have a quick chart at the bottom that compares several similar items and their specifications. The idea here is that if the item is lacking in one way, the customer may find that you sell a solution that is more suitable to them as well.

Proofread and Edit

After spending a bunch of time developing content, you really should take the time to proofread and edit all the ideas you write. If your English skills are lacking, it may be cool to find an editor to work with. Having a clean copy shows customers that you take your business seriously, and it helps to position yourself as an intelligent addition to the niche. Do not skip this step even if you've spent an entire week writing product descriptions and you almost burnt out on the process.

Revise Later

Much along the lines of editing, keep in mind that there may come a time where it's appropriate to update or improve your listings, especially if a product is reconfigured or otherwise changes. In the case that some of your content is time sensitive (i.e., mentions the year of manufacture), it may be wise to update these items as well. While this may not apply to every item, taking the time to occasionally update popular selling items' description could help you continue to make sales in the future.

Be Honest

The last bit of advice concerning actually generating the content for your product listings may be among the most important. The days of quack doctors and snake oil salesmen are over! Being dishonest about a product can and will come back to haunt you in the way of returns, bad reviews, and losing returning customers. Dishonesty can destroy your money-making prospects now that researching a product has become as simple as asking Siri for reviews on it. If you've taken the time to find great products, you don't need to sell them in dishonest ways or by overloading your product descriptions with unrealistic adjectives and claims.

6

_____

6 [6] https://www.oberlo.com/blog/write-epic-product-descriptions

Listing Products

Should you have taken the time to create compelling product descriptions first, then the process of listing your products becomes much simpler. The process is similar for most platforms, but there are some considerations involved. Since we can't possibly cover every e-commerce solution, we'll focus on the most popular: Shopify, Amazon, and eBay.

eBay

The great thing about dropshipping through eBay is you can list a product the same way you would if it weren't dropshipped. Just be sure that the shipping information and cost is setup correctly based on the supplier. For this reason, it's often ideal to work on multiple products from one supplier at a time and use some method of keeping tabs on which products are available from whom. So, it shouldn't be an enormous problem to incorporate this into your eBay efforts.

One facet of eBay listings to consider is that they no longer allow for "active content" within the product descriptions. This means you cannot embed videos, animation, or other "active" content that relies on software like JavaScript, Flash, etc.

Make sure to take the time to calculate the final value fees and listing fees as well, as these costs will eat away at your profits if poorly managed.

The huge downside to eBay is that there exists a lot of competition, but the upside is that it doesn't require extreme marketing. In fact, it doesn't require any marketing if you go the route of loading many products. The lack of marketing is really the only reason to use eBay over your own e-commerce solution. Of course, there's no reason you can't offer products through multiple channels.

Amazon

Listing on Amazon is a bit different than the other two platforms for a number of reasons. First of all, your product is most likely going to become part of a listing that already exists, meaning that all of your content isn't as useful as it would be on the other platforms. If you're only going the route of Amazon, this may be a relief because you simply won't need to produce as much copy. On the other hand, your competition is literally above or below you on the list of sellers, so if your seller rating takes a hard hit because of supplier errors in shipping or bad customer service on your part, it may quickly become an uphill battle to continue selling in amounts that are worth your efforts.

Listing Items Already Available on Amazon

What you can do is make sure to use the "Condition Notes" section to spell out those special "added value" points that you've painstakingly discovered by understanding your niche. You can also add in your own pictures of the product.

By now you know the prices, so adding in a price should be a pretty easy thing to do once you factor in the amount of cash you have to charge to make a profit. Keep in mind that there will be Amazon fees on top of all the other costs involved in selling this product. It is obvious that you will not be able to offer the lowest price, but this doesn't always mean you won't make sales. For shipping, you will need to determine this based on the supplier's methods and average shipping times.

Much like eBay, the downside to Amazon is the mix of fees and your competition being widely available all around your own listings. The upside is that there's not as much need to market your products, especially if you're able to price them fairly.

There are automated and semi-automated methods of handling Amazon listings for dropshipping, and Shopify specifically integrates Amazon into its system, making cross-platform sales fairly easy. The major problem with this is that the Amazon fees will cut into your profit margins, so it's imperative that you're sourcing items that can be marked up fairly significantly.

Creating New Product Listings on Amazon

If the item you're selling doesn't already have an Amazon listing, you'll need to pay for the professional Amazon Seller Central account to create new listings. This is about $40 per month, but because selling without the professional account adds a $0.99 fee to each transaction, it quickly becomes worth the cost if you're selling 40 or more items on Amazon per month. If you're creating your own listing, all of that work involved in copywriting your product description comes back into play.

The one thing to consider about creating your own listings is that you won't have the product on Amazon to determine if it will be an item that should sell well. It is more of a risk during the product research stage to keep this type of item in your potential "inventory," but because dropshipped items don't come with any significant overhead involved in purchasing items prior to sales, it may be a risk you're willing to take if you have reason to believe a product will sell. As a beginner, it is not recommended to start listing new products. By the time you are ready for this, you'll want to learn about the ins and outs of Amazon selling.

Shopify

Shopify (or another e-commerce solution) should be your focus in case you want to create a store that services a specific niche and brings in the best possible profits. Unlike Amazon or eBay, there are no sales fees for using the service; you just pay for monthly access and normal credit card processing fees.

When listing dropshipped products on Shopify, the ideal

situation is that you've already created all your content. This will make it easy to drop in the information, pictures, and prices. One of the great things about Shopify is that the product description is an open game, and there aren't limits on what you can include. The process is fairly simple, and we will discuss more of this in the later chapters.

Shopify has many tools to help with the automation of some aspects of your business, and their advanced reporting tools make it much easier to keep track of your business and profits.

7

Creating A Brand Logo

A very important piece of your business is the brand logo. You can't find a successful business without a brand logo because it is essential to building trust and legitimacy in your business. The logo defines your company.

---

7 [7] https://www.amzfinder.com/blog/list-products-amazon-complete-guide-fba-sellers/

How to find a brand logo?

The easiest and cheapest way to have a brand logo is if you or a friend have designing skills. You can simply design your own logo, or tell a friend what you want.

Having someone you actually know design your logo is a lot better than hiring a stranger because your friend can relate to you. They will have more knowledge of what you actually want which will improve the quality of your logo.

If you don't have a friend that knows how to design a logo, then your next best bet will be a freelancing site. You can hire freelancers to design a logo for pretty cheap on sites like fiverr.com.

On Fiverr, designers will work for you for as little as $5. Realistically, you'll be paying $6 because Fiverr charges $1 to process the transaction on their site, but hey, that's business.

Fiverr is the site that I use because it's worked great for me, but it may not be everyone's cup of tea. If not, you can try upwork.com which is another great freelancer site.

Although paying $6 for a logo sounds amazing, I recommend spending a lot more because the brand logo is the face of your brand. When people think of your service, they are going to be thinking of your logo so it must be high quality and professional. People will always associate your brand with the logo so, make sure it's something iconic.

8

---

8 [8] https://www.dropshiplifestyle.com/make-drop-shipping-business-stand-visual-branding/

Building A Website

There are tons of videos and books on the internet that explain how to make a website from scratch.

Just be prepared for the large amount of work that it's going to take because you are learning a new skill from nothing.

It'll take far longer for you to make your first sale this way, but the time invested in building any skill is not time wasted.

Alternatively, you can choose to use a website development company. Website development companies will make the website building process a lot easier if you're designing your own site because they streamline the process for you and make it more consumer friendly.

It's important to build a website that is pleasing to the eye because you cannot risk to set off any red flags in your customer's heads.

Customers are like birds. You need to throw them the bread crumbs and earn their trust slowly. Eventually, as the bird begins to trust you more, it will eat the bread crumbs closer to you until finally, it is eating out of your hand. If at any point you spook the bird, it will fly away faster than it came.

It's beneficial to keep in mind this bird analogy when making up your website. Don't cut any corners and make sure the website is well put together. Go the extra mile, and design your store to outshine other stores by adding your own little flair and creativity to it.

This is a must if you want any chance of your trade being a success. Open your mind, and realize that no cookie cutter formula will ever make you rich. Your success is entirely up to you.

You can also just hire someone to build the site for you, but this is much more expensive. Sometimes, hiring a professional who has been around the block a couple of times (definitely a lot more times than you) is the best path to success. This is especially true if you lack the skills required to design a website on your own.

Marketing Your Products

Free Traffic

In the age of social media (now), it is the perfect time to open up an e-commerce store. Social media sites offer places where people who share similar interests can form a group online and converse about it with each other. To set up an account is free and to post content and attract a following is also free. What a time to be alive!

If you want free traffic, you need to be providing value to people on social media. Whether it be fun or information, you need to be providing something to get people to want to follow you. Once you have loyal followers, they will see all of the content you put out including the occasional plug to your store or your products. This is the best way to control traffic and sales to your store with absolutely $0 invested.

This strategy can be used on any social media platform. Some of these platforms include Facebook, Instagram, YouTube, Twitter, and Pinterest.

It will take a lot longer to build a following of your own. Nonetheless, there are strategies to invest money into a social media platform to increase the traffic to your store. Regardless, you should continue to seek out new and better ways to provide value to people because you want them to stay interested and return for more.

Paid Traffic

Building off of social media, the quickest way to control traffic to your store is with influencer shoutouts on Instagram. The great part about this is it will increase your own following as well.

What you do is you make an Instagram page for your brand, and you post content related to your niche. So, if you want to sell kitchen appliances to people, you post a bunch of photos and videos about kitchen appliances on your Instagram page. You also need to leave the link to your website in your bio. Then, you pay an influencer in your niche to post an ad on their page.

This ad will be seen by the thousands of followers that this influencer has, so it's important to pick an influencer who has an audience that is interested in your niche. So, if you are selling kitchen products, the influencer you choose should be putting out content related to kitchen items because it will attract people who love such products. The ad will feature a link to both your Instagram page and the actual item in the store, so we're directing the traffic to where we want them to go and hopefully pique their interest.

This is a competitive strategy used by many other e-commerce businesses because it works. Piquing the customer's interest by first providing them with some value, and then marketing our product to them once they like and trust us is the best one-two punch combo for any e-commerce business.

9

---

9 [9] https://www.quora.com/How-do-I-market-my-dropshipping-business

Building A Brand

Growing A Following

Growing your following is a never-ending process because you can always reach more people. It is also an exponential process. In the beginning, your following may grow very slowly but as it continues to build, it starts to snowball. The more followers you have, the more social proof it is, and also the more likely someone is to have a positive image of you, leading to them following you.

If a random individual on the road tried to sell you something, you would most likely turn them down. On the other hand, if a renowned business with hundreds of thousands of followers on social media tried to sell a product to you, you would be more likely to buy from them. Subconsciously, seeing that this business has hundreds of thousands of followers makes you think that they must be doing something right, and they are trustworthy because so many other people seem to think so.

Consistency

It's crucial to be constant when it comes to branding. People like to see consistency in a brand because it paints a picture of you as reliable. Nobody has to say that you're reliable; it's just a subconscious judgment that people will make when they see your consistency.

The difference between two businesses who are both one year old is going to be consistency. Business A updates their social media, improves its website, and updates their products every day. Business B updates their social media once in a blue moon, improves their products at the beginning, and left their website as is. Both businesses are one year old, but Business A sees a lot of success and growth while Business B feels like it isn't going anywhere.

Building a business will take time but the amount of time it takes will be cut down by how consistent you are with it. Dedicate yourself to your business and make improvements every single day. Rome wasn't built in a day. Building something takes time, effort, and consistent improvement. Rome started out with one building, then two, then eventually it turned into what it is today. Begin building your Roman Empire.

The Benefits Of Building A Brand

As time moves on while your brand continues to grow, you will become more recognized and reputable. Here are a couple of benefits from building a brand:

Loyal Customers:

Customers will return to your store to buy from you again and again. Over a customer's lifetime, you can make hundreds upon thousands of dollars off of one person.

They're the first visit to your store they may buy $10 worth of stuff. Then the next time they visit, they buy $50 worth of stuff. Next thing you know, over the course of a couple of years, that same customer has purchased over $1000 worth of stuff from your store.

And that's just one customer. Think about the thousands of other loyal customers you will have and apply that same logic. That's right, money baby $$$.

The power of word of mouth

Different people will begin discussing your brand. Without having to ask them, previous customers will recommend your product to family and friends because they love your services so much.

In a survey, consumers were asked to fill out a questionnaire, and what was discovered is that customers are most likely to buy something if it is recommended to them by someone they know personally. Now your loyal customers are selling your products and services for you! How great is that?

Higher Price Margins:

You can demand a higher price for your products/services. A great example of this is Gucci. Gucci is a designer brand that is constantly idolized. Lots of word of mouth marketing goes on among consumers, and Gucci knows this. So, they charge high prices for their products.

A shirt that may cost them $5 to produce might be sold for $500. Customers are happy to pay this price because the clothing is Gucci-branded. The same shirt could be sold for $15 with no Gucci brand, and no one would ever go near it.

Your goal should be to improve upon your brand so much that people are no longer buying your products, but they are buying your brand.

Longevity:

Brands are known to stay around for a very long time. Designer brands like Gucci have been in business for years and will continue to do business for years to come. The only thing that could cause your brand to fail is another brand overshadowing it by providing better products or services that make your brand obsolete (Amazon.com ran Toys R Us out of business).

Competition:

You won't have to worry on matters relating to competition with other dropshipping stores. As a matter of fact, your brand will continually crush smaller stores. Your brand will be the big fish, and other smaller stores will be the little fish. Stores will have to work around your brand to see success. This makes your life much easier.

Dropshipping product pricing strategy

Dropshipping is a business model and e-commerce trend with high-profit potential and relatively low efforts. To be successful, you really should have a sound pricing policy. It is imperative that you determine your dropshipping pricing policy appropriately.

As a dropshipper, your only source of revenue is the difference between the prices offered by the suppliers and the prices that you set. This distinction is crucial, so you need to make sure that it is well thought out. You also need to ensure that you price your products right to be successful.

Getting the Price Right

Every entrepreneur grapples with the challenge of pricing their items. A nice pricing strategy gives you a room to understand the point at which you can increase your profits in relation to the sale of your items. Ideally, when you consider all the essential factors, you should be able to easily make the correct decisions and price your products appropriately for maximum profits.

Of course, at this stage, you still have plenty of questions on your mind. For instance, you may wonder how to determine the reasonable price of an item and how to get out the real value of a product in your store. There are a number of important factors that you will need to consider. Such factors include your customer base, the competition as well as your distribution costs.

Pricing Strategy for Your Shopify Store

This is a method that you use to price your products appropriately. The price strategy aims to enable you to maximize profitability while maintaining your customers. Pricing offers you the most efficient way of optimizing your store's potential. If you apply a good strategy, your store will remain profitable, efficient, and sustainable in the long term.

On the contrary, if you do not use a proper strategy to determine your pricing, then you will get into trouble. You might price your products too high or too low. This will cost you because you may lose customers who will seek lower prices elsewhere or you may not make sufficient profits to remain in business. Your customers may even suspect your products to be of poor quality.

The reason pricing is so important is because it is one of the major decisions that customers have to consider when shopping online. It is believed by consumer research firm PWC that most customers visit online stores just to compare prices. Other reasons include participate in promotions or to find coupons. In general, customers are always searching for great prices and, when applicable, discounts, vouchers, and coupons.

10

---

10 [10] https://www.shopify.com/blog/how-to-build-a-brand

Best Dropshipping Pricing Guidelines

Find products that cost less than $4 if you can

It is much easier to convince customers to purchase a product that is worth $4 or less compared to a pricier one. For instance, it is easier to convince a customer to purchase beautiful earrings that look great on her, match different outfits, and cost about $2.75 than sell her a designer bag worth $400.

Give customers discounts, offers, coupons, and deals

Everybody loves discounts, deals, and offers. The best approach is to keep your prices high at the beginning. Then, once you feel like you are no longer a new entrepreneur and are established, you can offer discounted product prices and coupons. These awesome deals can be offered to your customers. It will result in hordes of new customers visiting your online store regularly. Therefore, varying your prices a little can prove to be an excellent pricing technique for your online business.

Aim for zero shipping costs

As an online entrepreneur, you want to find products that have no shipping cost whatsoever. Ideally, you should mark products on your site as close to cost price as possible. Customers dislike shipping costs and will try to avoid these whenever possible. Find suppliers who provide free ePacket services. Many of them do, so try to find one who is trustworthy within your niche.

Flash the psychological card

It is usual practice by retailers to use odd numbers because customers prefer prices ending in odd numbers. Try to always mark your prices with odd numbers at the end such as $5.99. Your customers will round off this figure as $5 and not $6. Although this may seem a bit strange, it is a strategy that works. You should implement it at your store, and see how well it works.

How to handle returns

You will definitely love it anytime you sell and make a profit. However, returns will really bother you. Returns are always depressing for dropshippers. However, this disappointment can be a blessing in disguise. Always try to assist the customer where necessary. Focus on making the customer happy and avoid getting stressed. If your customers are happy, they will come back and will be happy to pay higher prices in the future.

Choose products with multiple variations

It is important to identify a product that comes in different variations. This makes it easy for customers to choose as they love variety. It also works pretty well with the Free Shipping cost model.

Use Simple but Powerful Phrases

It is important that when pricing your products, you make use of powerful phrases. Such phrases have a powerful impact on customers and will entice them to buy your products. For instance, use phrases like, "Get your adorable wristbands for FREE for a limited time only. Simply pay for Shipping!"

You should also let the customer know how long it will take before they receive their products. This revelation is essential for as a sales strategy. You can let them know that it will probably take 4 to 7 days for delivery. Customers love it when they have this information upfront.

11

---

11 [11] https://www.oberlo.com/blog/pricing-strategy-for-ecommerce

Chapter 4: Buyers' Psychology

How to Handle Your Customers and Provide Exemplary Customer Service

The biggest thing to remember when you want to create a long-lasting and sustainable dropshipping business is to keep a positive relationship with your buyers. All these aspects are going to come down to the encounter that your customer has with you and your product. Sometimes, you will find that it is tricky to maintain that trust with your customers since the whole business is done online, and there is no person to person interaction with your customers.

But when you are starting your dropshipping business, you ought to take the reigns and all of the responsibility for how well the customer service of your business is handled. Your suppliers are the ones who will take care of fulfilling all the orders. And if you picked a good supplier, you should find that part of the process to be good. However, the supplier wouldn't in any way have any contact with the customer. This means that you have to be the one who provides good customer service in order to keep your business growing strong.

You are the One Responsible

The first important thing that you need to keep in mind with this business is that no matter how well it is all running, there will always be moments when things will go in an unexpected manner. This can happen even for the best companies out there. Even the most trusted suppliers will run into trouble on occasion. But in the dropshipping business, when this does happen, you are the one who needs to go through and fix that situation.

In some cases, this may imply that you will lose some money to fix an order. But this loss of money will surely pay off in the long run. Fixing the mistake, even at a cost, means that you will have a customer who is more likely to get back to you. And they may even leave a more favorable review, rather than a bad review, to help your business grow a bit more in the future.

Understand Your Customers

If you can understand the wants and the needs of your customers well, then this will be a big factor when it comes to how well you are able to offer the buyer satisfaction in your trade area. The buyers want to feel secure when they shop with you. Making sure that your customers have a safe and secure checkout and that they will have their personal information safe when they shop with you can be very valuable to your customers.

In which manner will you achieve this? If you aren't using sites like eBay and Amazon, and you choose to sell on your own website, it is advisable that you build one that looks professional. Customers will run the other way if the website doesn't look professional and looks like it has been thrown together (this is a big sign of someone who is out to steal their information). In addition, on your personal website, you should consider adding in some extra security features to show customers that you value their personal information.

Know About Your Products

Customers are never happy when they procure a product, and it comes in completely different from what they expected. It is obvious that the buyers will be mad at you and possibly even leave a bad review if they end up getting something that wasn't what they expected at all. It is important to provide very detailed and good product descriptions to your customers and take pictures that actually showcase the product well.

Moreover, you can add in a few other parts to help answer any questions that the customer may have. Starting an informative blog, making sure there is a good FAQ page on the website, and even sending out a newsletter on a regular basis to explain products and other information can be helpful to your customers. Remember, the less a buyer has to come to you to ask a question, the more comfortable they are going to feel when they make the purchase and the less work you have to do. If you offer the knowledge for free, the customers are going to appreciate that, and they will see you as more of an expert on those products and that niche.

Happiness is the Top Priority

And finally, remember that a happy customer is the best when it comes to growing your own business. Transactions that are successful and have very little friction are going to lead to happy customers. Happy customers are most likely to get back to you, leave positive reviews, and tell their friends about the product. All of these things will lead to the growth of your business, and thus, you will make more money.

As you are working with your customers and creating a good experience for them, remember that a happy customer can be one of the top tools for marketing your brand out there. Treating your customers well and making them happy can help you to get your business out of there. It will also help your business grow much better than it would with any of the other tactics that we have discussed in this guidebook.

An unhappy customer can do the opposite. They will still leave reviews and share information about you with their family and fellow friends. But often, this information will be in a negative light that you do not want. Negative utterances spread faster than positive utterances. So, take the customer service of your business seriously and try to avoid any problems before they happen. And if these problems do happen, and they will at some point, do your best to handle them in a way that can satisfy your customer.

Customer service is completely your responsibility when it comes to your dropshipping business. The art of always taking care of the customer and your willingness to handle any of their questions, complaints, and concerns can make a big difference in how the customers feel when purchasing from you, whether they will share information with others about the business, and also if they will become repeat customers.

How to deal with competition

When it comes to dropshipping, you will see there is plenty of competition everywhere. Not only are there other companies selling the exact same product which you are selling, but there are as well other individuals selling those products and other similar ones that can fit the same type of demographic like you. It is important for you to search for some techniques that enable you to stick out from others to get customers to find you and to ascertain that you will get them to come back.

There exist distinct methods that you can use to make this happen. And often, it will depend on the products that you are promoting and the kind of business plan you follow. One thing to note is that lowering the price too much is usually not a good method to use. Yes, it may mean that you can offer a price that is much lower than what the competitors can do, but this often backfires. Many customers will be worried about why you price so low, thinking that you are selling a low-quality item. This can destroy your sales. Plus, when you price things lower, you can end up with lower price margins, and it is harder to achieve the profits that you want.

It is better to find other methods that can make you stand out from the competition, methods that show that you are ready to provide exceptional products and customer service to all of your customers, without having to hurt your bottom line too much.

One option that you can consider is starting a subscription service. If your product lends itself well to this, you could offer a discount to customers who agree to sign up for a few months of your service or product. This is a good strategy to get repeat customers and can make things easier for the customer since they can continue to have the product sent to them automatically when they need it each month.

Basing on the kind of supplier you choose to use, you may want to add something special to the packaging that you send out to the customer. Adding in a personalized note to it or finding a way to showcase your business entity can go a long way for you to showcase your work and feel like there is that personal touch. If you are unable to do this with your supplier, another option would be to acquire the email address of the customers and send them a personalized message in this manner. This helps the customer to feel valued and provides you with the start of your own email list that you can use later.

As a business owner, you will soon find that positive word of mouth can go a long way in growing your business. In the case a customer takes the time to share your products with their friends and is willing to talk up the product, then you are most likely to achieve big sales in the coming days. You can choose to use this to your advantage to make more sales.

When a customer finishes their order, ask them to share the word. You can ask them to refer a friend or place a little advertisement on Facebook or another social media site talking about their experience. Many businesses choose to offer discounts, such as 10 percent off the next purchase if their customers are willing to do this. It may cost a bit out of your pocket, but it can result in a high number of sales if you can get a few customers to choose to help you out. It is all worth the investment as well.

With some types of products, you may find that it is helpful to put add-ons with it to sell more. You can offer it as a special gift that goes with the product or make some bundle deals to help make things easier for your buyers when they are purchasing items. Buyers love the art of saving money on their purchases, and they love one-stop shopping. If you can provide them with a place where they can get several items that they need in one place, and you can offer your customers a discount on buying the items altogether, you can earn a big profit in the process as well.

Any time that you can add some freebies in with your sales, you should consider doing it. Maybe if you are selling a technology item, send a pamphlet with tips on how to use it, or send them your own personalized manual to help them use the item. It can make a difference. Or, if you are selling an item for making life easier in the kitchen, you can also send out a recipe book with the product to your customer. The point here is that you need to find some ways that you can differentiate yourself from the competition.

There will always be different people out there selling products, and sometimes, they will even sell the same product that you are selling. You have to find a way to provide more value to the customers than that which they are getting from the competition, or they have no reason to choose you over someone else.

If you are unsure of ideas on how to set yourself apart, go and look at what the competition is doing. See what the best sellers are doing in your industry and decide what you like and don't like, then implement these ideas into your own strategy. You will be amazed at the different things that other competitors are doing in your industry, and sacrificing the time to learn from them a bit can really help you to see the best results in your own dropshipping business when you first get started.

Providing good customer service can be very important when starting your new business. And this customer service definitely comes in a bunch of different shapes and sizes. If you are able to provide an exceptional product at a good price and identify other means to outdo the competition on the same or similar items, then you are well on your road to seeing success when you get started with this business model.

12

---

12 [12] https://blog.dsmtool.com/customer-service-best-practices-drop-shipping-business/

Chapter 5: Advertisements

Marketing Your Dropshipping Business

Up to this point, we've put in a ton of work learning about our target market, finding suppliers, generating our product descriptions, and setting up a website or other accounts, but we still have to actually connect with customers and make the sale. This is the part that stops a lot of e-commerce entrepreneurs, but if you've had your sleeves rolled up and haven't burnt out yet, get ready for some more of that hard work that pays off because marketing takes a lot of consideration. There are many facets to marketing a dropshipping business, so let's discuss some of your options here.

Additional Search Engine Optimization (SEO)

We've already discussed how to integrate some basic SEO into your product descriptions, but this isn't the only task you can work on to improve the visibility of your e-commerce store on Google and other search engines.

Images and videos. Having images and videos will help to integrate your site into the image/video search options on Google. This is also another chance to add in another use of a keyword into the metadata of your files. Shopify, specifically, will help you do this as they include some tools along the way to help with SEO.

Backlinks. A backlink is a link to your website on someone else's website, and when you receive backlinks from websites with good Google reputations, it will slowly help to build your own reputation on Google. Sourcing backlinks can be difficult, but asking to trade links with those in your niche may be your best bet. Likewise, you can offer to write a guest post for other people's blogs that will link to your site. It is important to stress that you really want useful backlinks and simply purchasing them from a freelance marketer is usually a bad idea as their methods may not be effective.

More content is better. The more original content you have that is optimized for SEO and quality, the easier it becomes for customers to run into your website.

Technical considerations. Technical concerns like page load times, correctly-coded websites, and proper preparations to allow web crawling software to scour the pages are important factors in SEO that are easy for those of us that aren't tech savvy to miss. The best thing here is that Shopify takes care of these issues for the most part! If you've decided to host your own website, it may be wise to spend a bit of money having someone do an SEO evaluation that includes these concerns.

Social media interaction also helps with SEO. Not only does it help drive traffic, but integrating social media tools into your site allows users to share your content. As social media grows, Google continues to create ways to measure the impact of social media interactions with other websites, and those with favorable results are pushed higher on the page ranking on Google.

Blogging

Running a blog is a good technique for many reasons. It does not only give you an outlet to create more content to flex your SEO and draw in more people to your website, but it also allows you to expand upon your selling methods. For example, you can create a Top 10 Microphones list. Not only will every brand you mention be a potential keyword typed into Google, but top 10 lists tend to perform well with readers, and they give you a chance to offer some of your items in Mike's Mic Shop. If you happen to include products that you are not dropshipping, you can set up an Amazon Associates account, use the affiliate link, and start collecting another income, one that's essentially passive by collecting commissions on sales.

Blogging also gives you the opportunity to better demonstrate some of the items you sell in a way that meets your niche head on. Creating content that helps them make wise purchases regularly may keep them coming back, especially if you include some form of entertainment as well.

It also gives your business a personal aspect when you write about things related to your niche and its community without trying to sell them something. It goes back to creating quality content. Quality content brings in website views, and website views should translate into customers if you're offering good products, customer service, and prices.

Social Media

Your business should be involved in social media in a personal manner. The more you can integrate yourself into the community that makes up your niche, the better you will have to sell to them. Not only does social media give you a great place to post your blogs, share information relating to latest products, and associate on a personal level about the things that matter to those within your niche, but it also offers feedback in the manner you are handling business. If taken seriously, this feedback can help do wonders to improve your business' shortcomings and spend more time on its successes.

The option of buying ads on Facebook that can be laser targeted to the demographics your market belongs to is as well available. Well-written Facebook ads marketed to the correct demographics can bring in new traffic, help you receive that feedback you need to improve and translate to sales if you've listened to your customers and met their needs.

As with everything, content is king. Your interactions and offerings ought to be of high standard and rich in value. If you're using YouTube, you should create useful how-to guides involving products you sell, and if you're posting on Facebook, it should be more than simply pasting a link to some of your products. Spamming will never work.

Coupon Codes

Depending on your e-commerce solution, you may be able to generate coupon codes. This is definitely available through Shopify. While dropshipping doesn't always allow for as much wiggle room on pricing and discounts, passing out coupon codes successfully through all your platforms is an easy way to encourage sales. It also does not cost anything except some of the profit from your sales on products you haven't paid for yet.

Email List

Putting together an email list is a wise way to keep your customers up-to-date with developments in business, store, blog, and other involvements. The easiest way to build an email list is to ask customers directly. There are a few places you can do this:

- On a sidebar on your blog

- On a sidebar on your storefront

- Through social media

- In order-confirmation emails

- In the surveys you run for market research (make sure it's optional)

- Facebook and other social media (link to a site for sign up)

When asking people to sign up for your email newsletters, make sure to mention that you offer special deals such as coupon codes and unique content not found anywhere else. You can set up email lists with services like MailChimp.com.

Product Reviews

Allowing product reviews on your e-commerce site not only helps by generating new, original content, but it also encourages sales when it is positive. For this to work out in your favor, you must ensure that you're selling high-quality products. Selling junk items and allowing product reviews is a recipe for quick demise instead of the almost-as-quick demise of just selling poorly-manufactured goods. You can encourage customers to leave product reviews through order confirmation emails. Unfortunately, since you're not handling the shipping process, you cannot slip anything into the box asking for customer reviews that way. In some cases, a supplier may be willing to handle something like this on your behalf, but this is something you only ask if the relationship has been largely beneficial to everyone involved.

Paid Advertisement

Of course, there are also methods that will exchange money for exposure. The popular methods are Facebook Sponsored Posts and Google AdWords.

The good news here is that you've done half the work already during the market research and keyword research stages. You need to have an idea of what keywords draw a lot of attention and the least amount of competition. Targeting these keywords with your paid advertisements are the best way to maximize your return on investment. The better you can pay per click, the higher up and more often your ad will show when people interact with websites that integrate AdWords, on Google search results, and through apps.

There are also other paid advertising solutions that often go overlooked. The most important of these is probably Bing Ads, which integrates into Bing and Yahoo!, and is typically much cheaper than Google Ads but works essentially the same way with keywords and bidding on per click costs. While you may not get as much traffic, the cost per conversion is much lower.

Taking advantage of these paid ads may be the quickest way to bring in some traffic, but it's important to remember that all the other elements of your business must be high-quality for paid advertising to truly pay off in your favor.

Be Involved

The best way to sell online is to be involved in the community of people that belong within your niche. Not all dropshippers are going to this extreme, but creating a personal connection with someone encourages you to support them, and having the support of the community that you're servicing is not only rewarding on a personal level, but it is rewarding on a financial level as well. The true trick to marketing is simply helping other people, whether that's with something important or just helping them enjoy themselves.

13

13 [13] https://beeketing.com/blog/drop-shipping-business-marketing/

Chapter 6: Facebook Advertising

Communication is a basic human need. It is just as important to individuals in their personal lives as it is to marketers and entrepreneurs in their businesses. Because of social media, constant interaction has become a major way of life. Social media has indeed simplified communication, and with it, opportunities have been created for marketers to reach their target audiences.

Among all the social media platforms, there seems to be one clear winner not just in relation to the number of active users, but more importantly, the excellent tools and options it is able to provide for businesses.

Is Facebook advertising worth jumping into? Let's find out as we explore some of the most-known benefits and possible drawbacks of using this social media platform for your advertising requirements.

Advantages of Using Facebook for Marketing

Reach a wide audience

Facebook, undoubtedly, has the greatest number of active users among all social media platforms. It is unbeatable when it comes to sheer size and number. And, more importantly, these are active users, ready to engage and interact using the platform.

Excellent targeting options

Facebook makes a lot of targeting tools available that allow marketers to reach the right audience. For a marketer, this reduces your chance of wasting a lot of money reaching the wrong people.

Low cost

With Facebook, you can advertise for as little as $5 or even $1 a day. And because of the targeting options, you have a better chance of getting the most value per dollar spent.

Customer loyalty

Facebook allows marketers not only to reach more people and increase awareness, but it also provides them an avenue to keep their existing customers engaged to build loyalty and profitable long-term relationships.

Flexibility

There are plenty of ad formats available from single image ads to video ads. Advertisers can also use a carousel of images or tell stories about their brand.

Easy to Use

For the most part, it does not take a rocket scientist to figure out Facebook advertising. Undoubtedly, it does take some time getting used to initially, but Facebook provides all the necessary tools and information to assist marketers in navigating the features.

Innovation

One major reason as to why this platform has stood the test of time and keeps getting stronger is innovation. The Facebook team constantly comes up with new ways to modify user experience for better performance. The Facebook team also continuously develop new tools that make advertising on Facebook intuitive, easier, and much more attractive.

Possible Issues with Facebook Advertising

Lesser organic views

Facebook has changed the algorithm, so that brand message visibility is limited. This means that among a fan base, only 8% may be able to view your posts. While this is disappointing for marketers, it's actually a good decision that can be very beneficial in the long run.

What Facebook is trying to do is maintain the social aspect of the platform. This is what makes people keep on using Facebook to document their everyday lives, interact with friends near or far, get information from their feeds, etc.

Cost is an issue

Although the minimum cost of Facebook advertising isn't significant, the cost can still be an issue for advertisers with a very limited budget. There are other ways to reach campaign objectives with free tools. Although it will take much more time and more effort, it is worth considering and integrating with paid promotions in order to reach the best-targeted return on your investment.

Requires commitment

As with other social media marketing tools, Facebook advertising requires commitment and a lot of effort. Although Facebook provides the platform and the tools to allow you to market and promote effectively, how you leverage these resources at your disposal is entirely up to you. You have to put in an effort to learn. This book will help you achieve that objective.

Incredible Reasons to Use Facebook Advertising

As you probably already know, Facebook is an incredible social media platform. At the same time, it has paved the way for the success of many business startups. The wide variety of tools made available to marketers and business owners make it possible to reach new customers and engage them to build and maintain a lasting relationship. The best part (and a lot of people aren't aware of this) is that a lot of these tools are free.

Ranging from custom audiences to lookalike audiences, Facebook marketing tools offer plenty of features and options to connect with a vast network of audiences. Here is a list of Facebook tools and features for businesses.

Facebook Page

Packed with features such as Messenger chat and appointment scheduling, Pages is a great way for businesses to connect with potential customers. It can be used for showcasing products and services. Customers can also rate and add reviews about the business. The call-to-action buttons are great for inciting a positive response.

Page Insights

This analytics tool is valuable for businesses that signed up with Pages. It tracks and analyzes responses from customers including the count of likes. Business owners and marketers can also see exactly where those likes are coming from. Data like a content reach, daily post-breakdown, and visitor demographic profile among others are monitored. It can also tell you which particular sections of your Page people are actually responding to.

Pages Manager App

This app allows you to manage and monitor activity on multiple Pages via mobile. You can post updates instantly as well as respond to messages and comments. Through this app, the latest updates on Page Insights are also much more accessible. You can get the app on Android and iOS.

Messenger

This is a free app for texting and video calling. It also allows users to send payments. The platform has undergone many iterations and improvements that have proved useful for businesses. Among those updates include Messenger Links to Pages and Messenger codes that can be used for scanning. It also lets businesses create customized notes sent automatically to users who try to connect with them.

Canvas

Quality content is important in engaging customers. Canvas makes this possible. Through this free tool, still images can be combined with videos to create interactive content. In addition, Call to action buttons can also be incorporated. Multimedia ads produced with this tool can be opened to full screen when users tap on the ads.

Power Editor

This is an excellent tool that advertisers can use for controlling ads, campaigns, and ad sets. Multiple ads can be edited through the Power Editor, and this can be used across campaigns.

Ad Creation Tool

This tool can be used for something more than producing ads. It also lets advertisers control which audiences to show the ads according to age, location, interests, and other factors. A Facebook ad, for instance, can be used to provide store directions. It can also direct a user to download an app, check out videos, add items to the cart, or any other action on the advertiser's website.

Ads Manager

Creating ads is just the first part. Ads Manager allows you not only to manage ads but also to measure their effectiveness. You can check on the performance of each ad or monitor ad sets (i.e., multiple ads grouped together). You also get access to campaign tools like campaign media, audience insights, and custom audiences. For large campaigns, you can use the Power Editor.

Page Post Engagement Ads

In case you want to make sure that more people see, like, comment, and share the content on your Page, this is the right tool to achieve those goals. You can create an ad, pick your objective to "boost your posts," and then choose Page Post Engagement. Select the Page, and choose which post you intend to boost. This Facebook tool also allows you to include a website address and send it to people. You can even use a conversion pixel that will allow you to monitor the results.

Page Like Ads

This is an incredible tool you can use to boost awareness of your Page. To use it, create the ad, choose Page Likes from the ad tool, select the Page you intend to promote and begin building awareness of that particular page.

Clicks to Website Ads

Driving traffic is one of the most important aspects of marketing. You can use this tool to send more people to your business website through an ad. Upon creating the ad, choose "clicks to website," then add the website address where you intend to send traffic. It could be your website homepage, your online store, or a product page.

App Installs and App Engagement Ads

If you have an app, this is one of the best ways to promote it. You can use it to drive awareness and motivate people to have your app. Create an ad specifically for your app and through the App Engagement tool. You can link the ad to specific areas of the app from the registration page itself to the online store where visitors can get more details concerning the app and make a purchase. As the ad makes an appearance on News Feeds of your target audience, you provide them with an easy avenue leading to the app you're promoting.

Event Response Ads

Facebook changes the way you promote ads. Instead of creating an invite to your event as an ad, you can use this tool to get users to add your event directly to their Facebook calendar. Once added, they can receive reminders pertaining to your event. You can then monitor the figure of people who have responded to the event.

Offer Claim Ads

Creating an offer or a promotion through special deals or discounts is a great way to get people's attention. You can do this more effectively with Offer Claim tool. With this feature, you can set the duration of the offer, choose the audience, and select how many people can make a claim to the offer. To use this feature, create your promo ad, and set your campaign objective as 'get individuals to claim the offer,' and then select Offer Claims.

Video Views

Video ads can be more engaging for the viewers. The challenge is to create memorable ones. This tool proves helpful in this matter. First, create your video ad and set your campaign objective to 'get views from the video.' Upload the video, and carefully select an eye-catching thumbnail. This is the first thing people see even before they get to see the ads. It's an important part of creating an excellent teaser.

Local Awareness Ads

For a more targeted post, this tool allows you to select your locality and also set the age and gender of the target customers you would like to reach. All that's left to do to start sending these potential customers to your business is to add the Get Directions button.

Slideshow Ads

This is a feature that allows you to produce video ads easily and edit them. Because slideshows are generally lighter using less data, they can load faster which makes them more accessible to users. It is an important consideration when users are mobile and connected with low bandwidth.

Carousel Ads

Creating a story around multiple products can even be more effective. The Carousel makes this possible. It also allows you to showcase multiple products using one ad. You can take advantage of this feature by introducing the products at various angles and providing important details. To use this tool, choose multiple images in one ad when prompted to select how you prefer your ad to appear.

Dynamic Ads

People who have visited your website or Page, checked out your posts, or dropped by your Instagram have already shown interest. Dynamic Ads tool allows you to retarget them by presenting these users with relevant products.

There are some prerequisites to start using this feature, and they are as follows:

- A product catalog,

- A Business Manager account, and

- Facebook Pixel.

Once you launch Dynamic Ads, you can promote your business on Instagram and Facebook as well as use Audience Network to showcase your products exactly where potential customers are spending most of their time. We shall discuss more the Facebook pixel in later chapters.

Lead Ads

Facebook has simplified the process for users to sign up and get information from various businesses in the form of quotes, special offers, and newsletters. This is what Lead Ads are all about. Through this feature, you can build contact forms within your ads with pre-populated contact info including email addresses.

Canvas Ads

The Canvas app lets you create multimedia adds combining still images with videos and finishing it up with a call-to-action button. It is a more interactive way of showcasing your products. With it, users can run through a carousel of images, view them from various angles, and zoom in on them to access the details.

Instagram Ads

Instagram has many active users. It has a slightly small user base compared to the figure of Facebook users, but a combination of these two in your marketing plan can prove to be highly effective. If you use Instagram, you can manage them using the Power Editor and Ads Manager of Facebook.

Business Manager

Security and control are among the things that business owners are concerned about. With Business Manager, you can easily manage your Facebook assets from your Pages to your ad accounts. It puts all these things together (in one place), and the best part is, it doesn't cost anything to set up!

Facebook Pixel

Among the most amazing features of Facebook advertising is the Pixel. It is essentially a piece of code embedded on your website which will allow you to build your audience for all your ad campaigns, measure, and optimize them. Basically, when a user pays your website a visit, clicks on something, or take any kind of action, Pixel records and reports this to you.

In addition, the pixel will try to find and match the action to a Facebook user. In this case, you will not only know that someone went to your website, but you will also find out if the user took such action as a response to your Facebook ad. After that, you can choose to retarget this user using a Custom Audience.

Hashtags

Phrases and topics can become clickable links on posts either on your Page or timeline. Hashtags make this possible. It will then allow users to locate posts according to their topics of interest.

Custom Audiences

Custom Audience can be formed to run ads specifically targeted to users you know of. You can start doing this by uploading contacts from a data file or email list. You have the options of copying and pasting them or importing those contacts straight from MailChimp, Aweber, etc. Assign a name and set a description for your Custom Audience. To run ads for them, choose the Audience field, and select the name you created for the Custom Audience.

Lookalike Audiences

Should you yearn to increase your customer base, you can use this tool to find more Facebook users that match the traits of your current customers using pieces of information like age, job role, location, gender, and interests. To use this feature, proceed to the Ads Manager, and choose Audiences. Tap on the Create Audience button, and select a Lookalike Audience. From the Source field, choose the Page and Custom Audience you intent to manage and the conversion-tracking pixel.

Audience Network

This is a good tool for monetizing mobile apps and websites. It's basically a network of publisher-owned apps and sites where you can show your ads. People spend a lot of their time on Facebook and Instagram. But they are also spending time on other apps and sites.

Audience Network helps advertisers reach more of the people they care about in the other places where they're spending their time. With Audience Network, you can choose from various formats including banner, standard interstitial, and custom native units for video and display. Furthermore, Audience Network ads use the same targeting, auction, delivery, and measurement systems as Facebook ads.

Facebook Blueprint

Facebook offers a variety of avenues for you to promote your business and reach customers. You can explore more about what tools you can use and how to boost your results further by using the Facebook Blueprint. From this, you can select courses, and customize your training according to your business objectives.

14

---

14 [14] https://www.woodropship.com/blog/successfully-market-dropshipping-business-using-facebook-ads/

Chapter 7: Outsourcing

Once you have formed your store, identified your products, and priced them appropriately, you now have to drive traffic to your store and thereby get customers to buy your products. It is important to promote your products and the store on different platforms using a variety of methods. You need to do this regularly whether you are seeking your initial sale or have been in the business for a long time. It is always advisable to identify more ways of marketing your products.

There are many different and creative ways of promoting your products. We need to find the most suitable and effective marketing techniques, and use them to attract customers to your store.

- Email marketing
- Print media ads
- Facebook shop section
- Reddit advertising
- Affiliate marketing
- Instagram
- Pinterest
- Facebook audiences
- Blogging
- YouTube
- Gift guides
- Pop-up shops

Open a Pinterest Account

Pinterest is one of the most effective marketing platforms for selling your products online. Many Pinterest users claim that they would use the platform to find products to buy and services to use, thus making it an excellent platform to advertise your products. It is a free platform that is very popular with users, so it is imperative that you open an account there, and reach out to the thousands of active users.

Use Social Media to Reach Out to New Customers

How to Work with Social Media Influencers

Sometimes, updating social media sites and writing blogs can feel pointless if you have a pretty small audience. One way of getting a pretty large following and numerous sales leads is to connect with influencers.

Basically, influencers are websites or individuals with numerous followers online. The following could be on social media or niche websites. Basically, one message, tweet, or post about your products will send a huge flood of potential customers to your store.

How to Identify Influencers

A lot of time, new entrepreneurs are unsure how to identify influencers to contact them. Influencer marketing is a form of marketing that places the focus or emphasis on specific individuals rather than the target market. It is advisable to search for micro-influencers with 1000 to 10,000 followers within a niche than celebrity influencers.

You can use apps such as BuzzSumo to identify influencers in your niche. BuzzSumo is a powerful app that searches for key influencers on Twitter in any topic area, niche, and location. Once it identifies the main influencers within a certain niche, it follows them and then adds them to your Twitter list. You can choose to follow probably three or four of the major influencers. You will then be able to see what kind of content they share, review the information they share, and even read their posts. If you are happy with the influencers you find, then you can proceed to contact them.

Also, you can use the app Pitchbox to find influencers in a given niche instantly. If your niche is women's accessories, you can use Pitchbox to find influencers who are popular in this niche. Using this app, you can identify important influencers without any manual input, and then send them customized emails. Those who do not respond to your emails will be followed up.

How to Contact Influencers

Use video message to contact influencers

Getting noticed by influencers is rather challenging because they receive numerous messages, likes, and tweets from many of their followers and even entrepreneurs. You really need to figure out ideas of attracting their attention. For instance, you can come up with a superb video message, and send it to an influencer as a direct tweet. Take the case of Aaron Orendorff, a respected social media influencer. He receives thousands of messages daily, but a video tweet from an entrepreneur caught his eye, and they got talking.

Send influencers a personalized Boomerang message

Another great way of interacting with influencers is to send a personalized Boomerang message on Twitter. It is a free app from Instagram which allows you to send an animated GIF to anyone on Twitter. The app takes 4 of your photos and converts them to a 4-seconds looping GIF. This is also bound to catch the eye of influencers.

Share and then tag an influencer to his or her content

You should find an influencer's content and then share it with your followers. Remember to tag the influencer to the shared content. This is such an effective way of catching their attention yet only very few people use it.

Follow and engage an influencer regularly

Twitter is a pretty noisy platform with lots of tweets, posts, and messages. It is difficult to regularly keep up with an influencer or engage them. Fortunately, you can catch their eye by engaging their content frequently. You should read and respond to their posts at least once a day. This can sometimes be tedious and time-consuming so you can use Twitter lists. A Twitter list is a great way to find Twitter users' content and engage with the influencers. You can easily create a list of influencers by going to their profiles and adding them to your list using the drop-down menu.

How Much are Influencers Paid?

Influencers are crucial in any serious marketing venture. They are used by large brands and small traders alike to attract customers to their products and online stores. About 85% of Americans somewhat or totally trust recommendations and endorsements from people they know. It is always a challenge to work out how much to pay the influencers.

The first step is to define your store's objectives and goals in partnering with an influencer. Do you wish to rent an influencer's audience? Are you looking to form a long-term relationship that may include co-creating content? Does the influencer have a reasonable audience within your preferred niche?

All influencers are not the same, and some command bigger followings than others. Those with more than 250,000 followers definitely command a higher fee than those below that. Micro-influencers may not have as many followers but definitely engage their followers a lot more and with more useful content. Here is a list of average earnings for influencers":

Micro-influencers with less than 1000 followers earn $85 per post.

Influencers on average earn $270 per post.

Those with over 100,000 followers earn $765 per post.

Nevertheless, these figures are not cast in stone, and you can always negotiate with any influencers you wish to work with. Negotiated agreements tend to have a greater impact on your niche market than the general agreements.

Instagram Influencers

Instagram influencers are crucial to any business. Their marketing messages are subtle, so they don't feel like advertisements. Influencers are a great choice for your preferred business or niche because they post ads that don't seem like ads.

Find influencers who are the right fit and resonate with your business. This way, their story will resonate with yours. Such an influencer should also have followers who are potential customers. Therefore, start by determining who your target audience is. Focus on location, gender, attitude, social standing, age, and similar factors.

Your preferred influencer should be interested in your product and should have the same interest as you do in your niche or area of specialization. Sharing interests with an influencer is extremely important for your business.

You need to choose between micro and macro influencer. Micro-influencers often focus on a small niche but have very loyal followers. Macro influencers have much larger followings. Think about your store and its products and you will know who your preferred influencer is.

A crucial factor that you need to consider is the number of followers. A suitable influencer needs to have between 200K and 300K followers. Also, each of their posts should have high engagement with followers. When you identify such an influencer, see if they have ads on their page and how these ads are faring.

Influencers charge for their services. However, you need to be savvy and bargain for a fair price. Basically, you should not pay more than $25 to $30 for a 24-hour post.

Now, you are ready to contact the influencer. Simply send a message directly to the influencer, and let him or her know about your marketing needs. Ensure that you approve the price as well as the date. The best day to have your marketing message or postmarked is Sunday. Once this is agreed, prepare the ad, and then send it to the influencer. Provide a catchy description and also a direct link to your products.

Make Use of Facebook

There are two distinct ways to use Facebook as a marketing tool. You can opt for Facebook Custom Audiences or Facebook Shop Section. Facebook is accessed by hundreds of millions of users each and every day. The Custom Audiences offers an excellent way of marketing to a select audience. Your ads will be targeted to your website visitors and email subscribers. This method is very effective.

An alternative or additional tool that you can use is to open a Facebook Page and add a Shop Section to it. Using your Shopify store, you can use Facebook as a sales channel, and create your own Shop Section. This will attract plenty of fans and friends who then buy directly from your Facebook page.

How to Set Up Facebook Pixel

As discussed in chapter five, Facebook Pixel is an app or tool from Facebook. You need to insert this app into your website so that it tracks the conversions originating from Facebook. It also helps you to optimize your ads based on the data collected. Facebook Pixel works by triggering cookies which it places on your visitors that track users who interact with your Facebook ads and your website.

How to Create your own Facebook Pixel

·   Go to your Facebook Ads manager, and select "Pixels" from the drop-down menu.

·   Choose "Create Pixels," then go ahead and create the Pixel.

·   Give your Pixel a name, agree to the terms and conditions, and proceed.

·   Now add the Pixel to your website so that it is activated. You will also need to add some code to your web pages. Simply copy paste the code or use the Tag Manager. All these are accessible from Facebook Ads Manager.

·   Now just confirm that your Facebook Pixel is working properly.

How to Set Up Google Analytics

Google Analytics provides a free and simple method of tracking and analyzing all visitors to your store. Google Analytics helps to find out who these visitors are and what they are looking for. Here is how to use it to help improve your

· First, sign in to Google Analytics using your ordinary Google account.

· Find the Admin button on the sidebar, then create an account.

· Create a property using the drop-down menu.

· Then choose a website, and add your store's name and web address or URL.

· Select your time zone and indicate your industry.

· Get a tracking ID, then install it on your website.

As you wind up account setting, you will have access to various reports including organic search visitors, keywords used to find you, the source of your landing page, and even active users. You should read these and other reports that will be generated by your account for Google analytics.

Outsourcing from Google Trends

It is one of the best tools out there that you can use to find good niches because it can offer you great insights into people's interest in all sorts of products. Google is the biggest search engine worldwide, so it has data on a very large pool of prospective consumers.

You can use Google trends to find out what the popular product searches are at any given moment, how people search volumes for certain products and niches have changed over long periods of time, the geographical information of people who are looking for certain products, and if people are interested in certain products throughout the year, or the changes in interest are cyclical or seasonal in nature. You can use these data points from Google Trends to identify products that are on high demand and niches that people seem interested in so that you can decide whether to invest in them.

The Trend Hunter

Trend Hunter is often used to find popular products within specific niches, and it can be used to assess the viability of a niche when you are trying to set up a dropshipping company. It's particularly useful when you are interested in niches where products often go in and out of fashion, or they are frequently updated. It's also a great place to find niche ideas because it lists thousands of products, all of which are meticulously grouped into categories and subcategories.

If you are considering selling a particular product, and you are looking to expand your product list based on how closely other secondary products are related to your original product of choice, Trend Hunter is the perfect place to find products that may compliment your core product. It's also the place to go when you are interested in identifying products that you can vertically integrate with your current ones in order to increase your market share within a given niche.

AliExpress

AliExpress is by far the most popular supplier for drop-shippers who import products from China to the US and other western nations. It lists thousands of sellers from whom you can source your products, so it's a great tool if you want to identify products and select niches that have the potential for profit. If you want to use AliExpress for niche research, you have to visit the website and check the statistics of the products that you are considering for your e-commerce shop. AliExpress uses a star rating system to measure product quality. This means that you can use it to filter out products that are of a poor quality when you are considering several options within the same niche.

You can run a product search on AliExpress and sort your results by quantity in order to rule out products that are in short supply or those that don't have a big enough market to warrant large manufacturing volumes. If you sort your products by numbers, you can be able to rule out niches that aren't popular. You can also see how long product suppliers have been listed on AliExpress (this tells you if the product is profitable in the long run).

The most important parameter that you ought to consider when using AliExpress for your analysis is the percentage of buyers who leave positive feedback in their review of the products that you are considering for your dropshipping business. The closer the positive feedback is to 100%, the more you know that you are dealing with a high-quality product that has reliable distributors. The information you gather from AliExpress can also help you figure out how to price your product, whether or not to expect consistent sales, and if a particular niche is suitable for promotion through advertising and other means.

Amazon Tools

Amazon is the biggest player in e-commerce right now, so it's a great source of information when you are trying to analyze which niches you can use to generate some profit. Amazon has many categories of products, and you can use their system of categorization as a guide to finding out about rare products and niches. One of the best ways to stumble upon niches that are relatively unexplored is by looking at the Quirky and Unique as well as the Interesting Finds sections on Amazon. These are the categories where Amazon places products that don't squarely fit into some of their most-explored niches, so if you study the products that are listed there, you may be able to coin a new niche that not many entrepreneurs have considered them in the first place. This fact will offer you the advantage of being among the first people to specialize in that niche.

Researching Your Competitors

It's not enough to identify a niche that could be profitable. You also have to study the other drop-shippers who have already gone into that niche and to identify if there is anything you can do to gain an advantage from competing against them. If you find a great niche that already has hundreds of retailers competing for customers, you can try to carve out a micro-niche within that niche so as to attract customers who are very specific about the items that they want to buy.

Chapter 8: Order fulfillment and Warehouse

In this chapter, I am going to look at the dropshipping supply chain. It is the channels through which the product follows from the moment it is manufactured to the moment it gets to the customer. For this, we need to first take a look at the three most important players that are involved in the supply chain of dropshipping business.

The Manufacturers: They are the companies that make the products. In most cases, manufacturers do not perform sales directly to buyers. Rather, they direct the sales to retailers and wholesalers who buy in bulk. When you want to resell a product, buying from a manufacturer is the best way to go. Although, a good number of manufacturers have less purchase needs, which means that you cannot buy below a certain quantity of product. This implies that you have to stock the products yourself and re-ship to your customers when they order. For this reason, buying directly from manufacturers is not a very good option when your aim is to run a dropshipping business.

Wholesalers: These companies buy the products from the manufacturers in bulk, and then sell them to retailers at a slight markup. While wholesalers might also have a minimum purchase requirement, theirs is usually much lower when compared to that of the manufacturers. In most cases, wholesalers will have products from many different manufacturers. Some wholesalers sell strictly to retailers while others sell to consumers too. As a dropshipping merchant, the best option is to source your products from a wholesaler.

Retailers: This is any business that directly sells products to consumers. If you run a dropshipping business, you fall into this category.

You might be surprised that "dropshipper" does not appear on the list of players involved in the dropshipping supply chain. The reason is that dropshipping is not a role. Instead, it is a service. This implies that any of the above players can act as a dropshipper or dropshipping supplier. It is possible to find manufacturers who are willing to dropship their products directly to your customers. Similarly, it is possible to find a retailer who is willing to ship directly to your customers. However, their prices are not going to be competitive like those of a manufacturer or wholesaler.

This information is meant to teach you to perform due diligence when searching for a supplier. While many companies might claim to be dropshipping suppliers, it does not mean that they are giving you their products at wholesale prices. It only means that they are willing to handle the shipping on your behalf. To be sure that you are getting the best possible price, you should ensure that your supplier is a legitimate manufacturer or wholesaler.

What to Look for in a Good Supplier

In the dropshipping business, you expect to have a long and mutually beneficial relationship with your supplier, so make sure that you pick one with whom you have great chemistry. That means that you need a supplier whose staff is always professional and knowledgeable in matters that are related to your specific niche. You should be able to call them for information if you have questions about the product. Your supplier should also be well staffed. As a valued partner, they should assign you a dedicated sales representative who will be responsible for handling your account with them. This will help ensure that your problems are dealt with promptly, and when you log a complaint, it never gets lost among many other messages that the supplier receives on a daily basis.

You should also find suppliers who care about integrating modern technologies into their systems. Technology helps to automate dropshipping businesses, and it reduces the tasks which you have to perform. Technology also reduces the chances of human error during the order fulfillment process. Make sure you prioritize suppliers who have real-time inventory management and detailed online catalogs. At the very least, your supplier should take orders via email—calling in one order at a time is just too labor intensive, and it negates the whole reason you went into dropshipping in the first place.

Identifying Fake Wholesalers

Fake wholesalers are a real thing that new dropshipping traders have to watch out for. There are lots of middlemen who are trying to make money from you, and unfortunately, they are the ones who invest in SEO and PPC adverts, so they often outrank legitimate wholesalers in search engine results.

There are some telltale signs which can bring to your attention the possibility that you are dealing with a fake wholesaler. If you find a wholesaler who is demanding that you pay a large monthly fee just so you can be allowed to make regular orders, you are probably dealing with a middleman. Real wholesalers don't need membership fees as a revenue stream because they make enough money performing their core business function, which is to buy from manufacturers and to sell to retailers at a markup. Also, beware of "wholesalers" who sell directly to the public, because they aren't really wholesalers, they are more like retailers.

The Order Fulfillment Process

A customer will get in touch with your dropshipping business and place an order for one or a number of your items. The customer will either reach out to you by telephone or use a checkout cart to place a purchase order on your website or sales page. You will then approve the order. If it's on the phone, you will acknowledge the fact that you have accepted the responsibility of fulfilling that order. If it's online, the customer will see a message confirming that he or she has indeed made a purchase. Both your business and your customer will receive automatically-generated notifications indicating that there is an order in place. The customer may get an email confirming his purchase, and you may get a notification (this is particularly important if your customer has placed the order over the Internet).

Make sure that you pay attention to your notifications so that you can take action immediately after receiving them. The customer's payment will be automatically received and deposited into your business account immediately after the checkout process is over. The amount the customer pays will be the price specified on the website for the product plus the cost of shipping (if it's indicated separately).

Order Placement by Your Business with the Supplier

You will use your business account to place an order with a supplier for the exact product that the customer wants. Most dropshippers set things up in such a way that this step would only require them to forward the confirmation email that they receive when the earlier step is completed. Usually, the wholesaler will already have your business credit card information on file, and he will charge the wholesale price of the product together with the shipping and processing charges to that card.

Some dropshippers make use of sophisticated programs that allow the orders to be sent to the supplier automatically, but most start-up drop-shippers don't have the resources to do that, so they just use email to submit orders to suppliers.

Order shipment by the supplier to the Customer

If no complication arises at this stage, for instance, in case the product is out of stock, or if the wholesaler is unable to successfully charge the card that he has on file, the wholesaler will take the product out of storage, package it as instructed, and then ship it to the customer's address.

The wholesaler won't print his business name or address on the package. Instead, he will print your logo, business name, address, and other contact information. The invoice that is sent to the customer along with the package will also contain your logo and letterhead, not that of the wholesaler's. When the wholesaler sends out the package, he will email you a duplicate of the invoice for that particular shipment, alongside the tracking information for the package.

Quality suppliers will have decent turnaround time—they may be able to ship out the order just a few hours after they receive the request. Same day shipping is a big selling point in e-commerce, so you should try to find a supplier who guarantees it.

Alert the Customer About the Shipment

When you receive the shipping information from the supplier, take note of the tracking number for the package and any other essential information, and then send it to the customer. You can send the tracking info via an email system that is built into your e-commerce site. Once the customer has the tracking information, the fulfillment process would be complete. The only activity that is left is for you to wait and see if the customer has any complaints (e.g., if there are delays in shipment, should there be a mix-up with the item, or if the item has been impaired during transportation).

There are a few conditions that must be met in order for a dropshipping fulfillment process to work correctly. Among the crucial conditions is that the wholesaler or supplier should remain invisible to the customer. Under no circumstances should the customer be aware of the fact that the fulfillment of his or her order involves another party other than you. If the wholesaler is revealed to the customer, the whole dropshipping charade will fall apart.

If the customer has a problem with the package that is delivered, he is supposed to get in contact with you and log his complaint. You will then turn around and relay that complaint to your supplier. Your supplier will take action to solve the problem, and then he will tell you what he has done, and how soon he expects the issue will be fixed. You will then call the customer and tell him exactly what the supplier has told you, but without making it sound like its someone outside your business that's actually handling the problem.

The system is cumbersome, but it's necessary for the dropshipping business model to work. If the customer finds out about your supplier, he might lose trust in you, or he might decide to remove you from the process and order directly from your supplier during future purchases.

So, now that you understand the structure of the supply chain and how the fulfillment process works, what actions can you take to ensure that the fulfillment process for your dropshipping business runs like a well-oiled machine? Well, there are a few actions that you can consider to increase the efficiency of your process.

For starters, you can try to automate most of the steps that need to be taken in the order-fulfillment process. For instance, you can make sure that it's very easy for your customer to place an order with you. Set up your e-commerce website in an intuitive manner, and reduce the number of clicks that are needed to make a purchase.

Make sure that the payment system for customers is straightforward. When the order comes into your business, make sure that there are automatic notification systems for both the customer and yourself. Also, you can choose to set up your system so that orders that come in from customers can go out directly to the supplier without you having to forward them manually. This will reduce the amount of effort that you have to put in, and it will minimize the risks of you failing to submit orders to suppliers because of mix-ups or human error.

Also, you should ensure that the card that you possess on file with your supplier has enough balance to cater for the cost of the orders that you are forwarding to him. If the supplier is unable to bill you for an order, he won't have any reason to fulfill it.

Chapter 9: Setting up a Shopify store

If you want to have your own presentable, unique, and high-quality e-commerce store with all essential features, then you need to set up a Shopify store. Without a doubt, Shopify is one of the most popular online platforms that provide e-commerce solutions for entrepreneurs.

Shopify allows you, at minimal cost, to build a modern, functional, and professional-looking store all by yourself. The stores are very presentable and of great quality. They are very similar to what any professional web designer would build.

What is Shopify?

Shopify is a premier e-commerce platform that allows entrepreneurs to create their own retail point-of-sale systems and online stores. It is a comprehensive, complete, all-in-one online trading solution. Shopify allows interested entrepreneurs to open an account and set themselves up. Once you open an account, you can do all the following:

· Design and create your online store by yourself

· Identify distinct amazing designs to select from

· Choose a catchy name and domain for your online store

· Add then display products complete with descriptions and prices

· Start receiving and processing orders from customers

· Begin handling payments through various payment solutions

· Decide if to run any promotions, give discounts, and sell products

In short, Shopify offers you a very cost-effective and affordable opportunity to create your own e-commerce business. The software on Shopify is constantly upgraded to modify it more in a more efficient manner and modern appearance which makes it more reliable in the long term. As an account holder, you get to receive excellent customer support 24-hours a day, every single day.

Key Features of Shopify

Once you form a Shopify account, you will gain access to a wide variety of tools. These tools will enable you to arrange and manage your business. There are different pricing plans offered by Shopify. According to the plan you settle for, you will be able to access several tools ranging from payments processors to themes and so much more. Here are some of these tools which you will gain access to:

· Paid and free applications from the Shopify app store

· Paid and free themes that you can acquire from the Shopify theme store to ascertain your website is exceptional and outstanding

· Payment processor from shopify to enable you to receive payments from credit card

· Access to a blog that gives you articles that guide you on how to successfully operate and manage your own business and connect you with customers

· Opportunities to grow and expand your business

· Enterprise plans for high volume entrepreneurs who prefer lower transaction fees

· Global experts who can advise and help design and market your online retail store

Open an Account with Shopify

The first thing to do is open an account. Visit Shopify's website at www.shopify.com, and find the Sign-up page. Open this page, and follow the outlined steps to form the account. There are some details required and once provided, simply tap on the link that says "Create your Store Now."

It is good that you come up with a unique name for your store. Shopify system checks all names you provide and only approves a unique store name. Other details that you will give out include your name, country of residence, address, and a contact number. Shopify also wants to know if you have products you wish to sell and, if so, which products these are. Once you provide all the necessary information needed for setting up your account, just tap on the tab "I'm Done."

Shopify offers you a free 14-day trial once you open your account. This allows you to arrange your store and test different things to see if and how they work without spending any money. At this stage, Shopify will require some details from you due to legal requirements. For instance, if you will be operating as a real store, then you will need to provide tax information and other relevant information.

Setting up your First Shopify Store

When setting up your first shop, you have to visit Shopify's homepage and look at the main dashboard. You will see plenty of buttons on the left-hand side. These include the following:

· Homepage button

· Orders

· Products

· Reports

· Discounts

One of the things that Shopify does is present you with an entire list of actions to take to fully set up, customize, and personalize your store before eventually launching it.

Shopify will then ask you what you intent to sell. Simply choose one of the options available from the drop-down menu. These include electronics, computers, fashion, and apparel, and so on. Let us choose "Women's Accessories" like earrings, wristbands, and necklaces, then proceed with this as our preferred niche.

At this point, you can start adding products to your store. The process is extremely simple. Click on an image then "drag and drop" it to the appropriate place on the dashboard. There is a button labeled "Add Product" button that you tap on to add products.

You should label your products in a manner that clients can identify with. This also makes things easier for you when uploading or referring to a particular product. However, many dropshipping entrepreneurs do not have their own products and rely on a dropshipping supplier. We will look at importing goods from suppliers later. However, if the product images are readily available, then you can upload using this simple method.

As soon as you finish, just click the "Save Product" button, then go to the homepage to see the products. The products can now be viewed and even purchased.

If you visit the dashboard of your homepage, you will be offered a number of options. Shopify wants to know where you want to sell the products. Alternatively, you can choose to create an online store, sell on Facebook, sell in person with a Point of Sale system, or even add products to an existing website. From these options, we note that the most viable in our case is to create an online store.

Find a Suitable Layout or Theme for Your Store

Shopify has its own themes, and you can search through them and select one. There are many colorful, great-looking, and presentable free and premium themes that you can use.

Now, all the themes at Shopify come with a guarantee that they have full support from designers. This is reassuring for users, knowing they can fully trust the themes. All the themes have a comprehensive array of modifications that you can apply without the need to do any programming. Premium themes have more functionality, but you can still do a lot with the free ones.

If you choose a theme but wish to make substantial changes to it, then you need not to worry if you cannot program. Apparently, Shopify has an excellent team of design experts from all over the world. These Shopify experts are available to members and can help you customize and make any necessary changes to your store. There are some pretty simple steps to follow if you are to find the best theme.

Browse the Shopify Theme Store

First, go to your homepage, and then tap on the "Themes" button. This button will take you to Shopify's theme store at www.themes.shopify.com. There are over 180 different themes to choose from. These include both free and premium themes. When browsing through the themes, you can decide to browse through the free or the paid themes.

Also, you can filter the themes by features and by industry. The themes can then be sorted by popularity, most recent, and price. Spend your time browsing through the themes until you find a couple that really impresses you. Do not rush this process because your interaction with your customers will depend on your store's outlook and presentation.

Look at the reviews and functionality of themes

Once you identify one or two themes, check out a sample image. When you do, you will also receive more information about the theme including its flexibility, adaptability, and responsiveness. Additional information lets you know whether the theme is mobile ready and how adaptable it is to modification. There are always reviews if you scroll down, so go and check out the reviews. These will let you know about the experience of other users and what their thoughts are on a particular theme.

Shopify has a cool feature that allows you to view any theme you choose in action. When you choose a theme, you will notice a "View Demo" button. Simply click on this button and preview the theme. This will show you how your online store will look like. You can also view demos on the different styles if your chosen theme comes in a variety of styles.

Get your chosen theme

As soon as you decide which theme you like, you simply click on it to get it. You will notice a green button which you need to press. Shopify will want you to confirm that this particular theme is the one you really want. If you agree, then the theme will be installed. One advantage you have is that this theme does not have to be perfect. If you feel, later, that you do not like it, then you can always change it and choose another one. To install your chosen theme, simply click "Publish as My Store's Theme." Once it is published, Shopify will let you know and will offer you a chance to change at any time should you change your mind.

Top Free Shopify Theme

Brooklyn is among the most popular free Shopify themes available and comes in two different styles. These styles are Classic and Playful. The Playful style is more niche-oriented and features brilliant colors, making it suitable for kids' toy store, ladies' fashion boutique, or even a chocolate store. The Classic theme is great for apparel stores and clothes retailers. It has excellent features, is user-friendly, and is very easy to use.

Brooklyn Shopify theme is well-suited for a modern apparel store. Some of its features include unique typography, product grid, homepage slideshow, and mobile responsive design. You should not worry at all about products displayed on the theme as these are just for display purposes. You will get a chance to upload your own products at the appropriate time.

Edit Store Settings

You probably do not want your store looking like any other online store. This is why Shopify themes allow users to make simple yet effective changes that can completely alter your store's appearance. Consequently, you can rest assured that your store will be unique and stand out based on the settings that you choose.

First, visit your homepage, and check out the admin screen. From here, click on "Themes," and you will see your live theme at the top. There are two dots next to the "Theme," both of which are settings that you can use. The initial one allows you to create a duplicate of the current theme which is a great idea, so that is what we do. The other button is for customization. Use this button to customize the theme according to your preferences.

Tap on the Customize Theme button, and you will be redirected to a page that enables you to control all the fundamental functions of your Shopify store. These controls give you an amazing opportunity to adjust the settings and take a look at the features, enabling you to explore in details what your store is capable of.

Customization allows you to change or do the following:

Change font

Determine the number of items to appear on each line on the collection page

Upload logos to the store

Determine your preferred color schemes

Add slides to the homepage carousel

Edit functionality on the product pages

With all these features and functions, you can easily make changes and adjustments to your store. This will make it unique, appealing, and user-friendly.

Use Oberlo to Add Products to Your Shopify Store

Once you are done with the design and setup of your Shopify store, you now need to add products. For you to seamlessly import and add products, you will have to download Oberlo. It is the leading app used by e-commerce entrepreneurs who wish to import products to their stores. Shopify and Oberlo are seamlessly integrated, making it very easy to start importing and adding products to your store.

What is Oberlo?

Oberlo is a popular app from Shopify. It provides a useful service that enables you to import products from the popular Chinese store known as AliExpress. As a dropshipper, Oberlo is ideally one of the best applications available to you. Using Oberlo, you can easily and seamlessly import thousands of products from AliExpress warehouse, and start selling to your customers.

The reason why Oberlo is crucial to Shopify dropshippers is that it saves them plenty of time and effort when adding products from AliExpress. Oberlo is currently being used in more than 6,500 Shopify stores and has more than 300 positive reviews. Oberlo works only with AliExpress and not any other wholesale stores or suppliers. There are good reasons for this so let us first teach you a little bit about AliExpress.

What is AliExpress?

AliExpress is a global wholesale and retail online marketplace developed and overseen by Alibaba, the world's biggest online marketplace. Anyone can place an order for wholesale items on AliExpress. You can also purchase a single item and still be protected by AliExpress Buyer Protection.

Buyers on AliExpress can purchase products directly from manufacturers. This enables them to get lower prices as they cut out middlemen. Buying directly from manufacturers ensures that buyers and dropshippers are guaranteed the lowest prices in the market.

Most people describe AliExpress as the retail section of Alibaba which provides a useful service to millions of traders, retailers, and customers all over the world. Alibaba on its own generates more sales than both Amazon and eBay when put together. The term express means that this service is designed for express, wholesale transactions.

The main target markets of AliExpress include small and medium-sized buyers and suppliers. This way, they are able to access high-quality products at very affordable prices. The minimum order accepted is a single item or product which is shipped via express delivery. Sometimes fast and free shipping is available to entrepreneurs.

Sign Up for Oberlo

There are two different ways you can use to sign up to Oberlo. The first is to visit the official Oberlo website at www.oberlo.com and sign up directly. The other option is to sign up through Shopify. The Shopify app marketplace listing makes it easy to sign up directly. The direct access is apps.shopify.com/ali.

In our case, we have already installed Shopify on our device, so we will click on the installation link that is provided. This link is highlighted on the homepage and is easily noticeable. Simply click on it and register. After installation, the app will appear on your homepage.

From here, you can begin adding products to your store. We will need to register a credit card on Oberlo to perform a trial run. Please note that Oberlo is not used for free. You get a 30-day free trial on the premium plan before moving to the lowest plan which costs $4.90 per month. For the app to be activated, you will need to approve this charge.

Benefits of Using Oberlo

The Oberlo dashboard is pretty easy to use. It also offers plenty of conveniences. You can access the Oberlo dashboard directly from the Shopify admin section. There is a section labeled "Get Started" on the dashboard that helps you accomplish certain tasks. For instance, it helps you set up pricing rules so that you know how to set prices the items.

Oberlo has plenty of simple video tutorials that help you understand how to set it up. For instance, you can watch tutorials that show you how to items, the way to import them to your store, and even how to connect existing products. Always bear in mind that your products form the most important part of your Shopify store.

Using Oberlo, you can search for products at AliExpress. There is a "Search Products" page where you enter different keywords to find the categories and actual products that you want. Oberlo also allows you to import products to your Shopify store using either the product ID or products URL.

You can also use Oberlo's Chrome extension if you want to import products as you browse AliExpress. If you lack ideas, then you can access a featured products page to get ideas. Sometimes, you have to search through numerous products to find the right one. Each product comes with important information such as product rating, price, sales figures, supplier information, and so much more.

Now that you have uploaded all the products to your store, you are ready to begin selling. Making sales and generating revenue is really what your Shopify store is all about. However, you will still have a lot of work to do because by simply launching your store, you will not necessarily attract any significant traffic. Therefore, you will also need to engage in suitable marketing campaigns to bring in potential customers. Keep trying different marketing methods until you find the one that works for your trade area.

Other Must-Have Apps for Shopify

Free Shipping Bar by Hextom

Free Shipping Bar is an app that provides a fully-customizable bar. It enables you to give out free shipping to your buyers to increase your sales. This app is simple to set up. It makes your site look organized and professional. It is an app that you definitely need for your store.

SalesPop

SalesPop is a powerful tool that helps you boost your sales. It is estimated that over 85% of store visitors never buy anything. Reasons for this include store authenticity, trust issues, engagement, and so on. SalesPop helps create an aura of a busy store which will entice customers to actually buy products at your store.

MailChimp

This is a useful marketing app with multiple applications. This app helps you capture emails from visitors and create a marketing list. You can then use the list created to send marketing messages, newsletters, and so much more.

Personalized Recommendations App

This is an e-commerce app for Shopify that promotes sales at your store. It suggests the right products to customers based on buying history and behavior. The app can tailor recommendations to every unique customer to your shop.

Countdown Cart

This app helps create urgency in customers. A lot of customers tend to delay buying. However, Countdown Cart helps convince buyers to go ahead and purchase products at your store.

Trust Hero

This app boosts the level of trust that customers have in your store. When you have this app activated, it will display trust icons at your store and reduce incidences of cart abandonment. Customers will gain trust in your store and will be happy to buy your products.

There are websites like hotjar.com where you can create heatmaps and see how visitors are using your site. You can collect useful feedback which you can use to turn visitors into customers. It also enables you to know if your site has errors.

15

---

15 [15] https://www.oberlo.com/blog/how-to-set-up-your-shopify-store

Chapter 10: Common mistakes to avoid when venturing into dropshipping business

Here are some common mistakes that many beginner dropshippers tend to make. We will discuss why people find themselves making these mistakes, and what you should do to avoid making them:

Starting Without Learning the Ins and Outs of Dropshipping

There has been much hype around the topic of dropshipping, and a lot of misinformation comes with the dropshipping idea. Many self-proclaimed "dropshipping gurus" have been telling people how swift it is to start a dropshipping business, and this has led a lot of people to assume that you do not require to learn any technical aspects of the business to succeed. The truth is that the dropshipping game is evolving pretty fast, and there is stiff competition in every niche, so you should avoid jumping into the business without taking a little time to explore as much as you can concerning the trade.

Choosing Bad Suppliers

Many newbies fail to look into the history of suppliers to find out if they have a reputation for unreliability. They assume that in order to maximize their profits, they need to go with the supplier who offers the lowest prices, but the truth is that the quality of service and the reliability of a supplier is much more important for a drop-shipper than saving a few cents on each order. If a supplier messes up and makes a lot of excuses during your first few weeks of operation, you should drop him and find a more reliable one before your business gets stuck with a bunch of negative reviews.

Lacking Faith in the Dropshipping Model

For you to succeed as a drop-shipper, you have to stick to the model. Some first-timers make the mistake of doubting how the model works, so they try to blend dropshipping with other forms of retail e-commerce. This often happens when newbie drop-shippers worry about their suppliers running out of stock, so they go out and use their own money to buy some inventory. If you have chosen to be a drop-shipper, you should stick with it, and concentrate on scaling your business, and you should avoid complicating things unnecessarily. Have faith that the system will work.

Expecting Money to Come Easily

Again, the notion that dropshipping brings in quick and easy money originates from the so-called experts who misinform people because of their own personal agendas. As a drop-shipper, don't assume that you will set up a store, launch it, then sit back, and start watching the money flow in. Success in dropshipping requires hard work, proactivity, and a competitive attitude. Customers don't just come to your shop;

you have to go out there on the internet, find them, and bring them in through advertising and content marketing. Dropshipping is not a get-rich-quick scheme.

Failing to Retarget Your Site Visitors

Retargeting site visitors is probably the most effective marketing strategy out there in terms of the sales that it generates. If you don't take advantage of retargeting ads on Facebook or Google, that's akin to throwing money away. People visit a shopping site or a sales page because on some level, they really would consider buying that product, so if you keep reminding them about it, one day, as soon as they can get some money, they are highly likely to come back and make that purchase. If you have limited marketing funds, make retargeting ads a priority in your marketing strategy.

Using Low-Quality Product Images

First-time drop-shippers are encouraged to use free photos as a cost-cutting measure, but that doesn't mean that you should use low-resolution product photos. If your supplier provides low-quality photos, try to find better photos of the product elsewhere online, or you can order a sample of the product, and take your own photos of it. Online shoppers don't get to see the products they are buying beforehand, so they rely on photos to make purchase decisions. To be fully convinced about the quality of a product, most of the buyers would want to see lots of high-resolution photos from different aspects so that they can zoom in and study the product in detail.

Misleading Your Customers About Your Shipping Time

Many new drop-shippers are afraid that the customer might go elsewhere if they think that the shipping time for a product is too long. Some drop-shippers are tempted to either conceal the real shipping time or to straight up lie about it. If you can't guarantee fast shipping for a certain product, you should be honest about it and offer an explanation as to why it's taking more time than expected (perhaps you are shipping it from abroad). Misleading customers about your shipping time counts as terrible customer service, and if a customer has to wait longer for a package that he was promised, he is highly likely to take his business elsewhere.

Being Afraid to Reinvest Your Money in the Business

When dropshipping novices make a little money from their businesses at the beginning, some are usually afraid of putting the money back into the business for fear that they could end up losing it all. However, the right approach is to reinvest at least some of the money you make into the business through advertising or SEO. There are lots of ways to advertise one's dropshipping business—you could hire influencers, buy PPC ads, etc. Your business won't grow if you take every cent you make out of it. Use your proceeds to scale your business in order to gain more profits.

Failing to Work with Instagram Influencers

As of now, Instagram is rated as the hottest platforms if you are looking to advertise any kind of product. People follow influencers on Instagram to an almost religious extent, and you would be surprised at the number of people who will be into the trend of buying a product just because one influencer mentioned it. You can easily find an influencer within your niche who is willing to give your store or product a shout out for a bit of cash. The bigger you dream, the bigger you'll grow, so don't be afraid to spend a lump sum of cash for an endorsement from a few powerful influencers.

Using Complicated Shipping Fee Structures

First-time dropshippers tend to publish complicated shipping fee structures on their websites or to display shipping fees under the price tag of every item in their shops. This can be confusing and off-putting for many customers. Customers don't need to see your cost breakdowns; they just want to know how much the whole thing is going to cost them. Instead of having separate shipping fees for all listed items, you should just set prices that account for shipping costs and then offer free shipping. This is a neat marketing trick that can make customers think that you are offering them a nice deal.

Creating Unclear Policies

Many novice dropshippers make the mistake of thinking that store policies are mere formalities, so they fail to make them as clear as necessary. You should avoid having unclear policies. If you don't know how to create such policies, you can borrow ideas from other similar businesses, or you can use online tools provided by industry players such as Shopify. For example, if you don't explicitly state in your policies that a customer has to include a tracking number when returning a package, and then the customer claims that he sends back the package without producing a tracking number to prove it, you won't have any recourse if the package "gets lost in the mail."

Mishandling Product Returns

Product returns are complicated and frustrating for drop-shippers because they require a lot of correspondence, and they cost money. However, they are also an opportunity for you to deliver good customer service, and they help you learn the weaknesses in your system so that you can fix them. Many first-time drop-shippers mishandle product returns by trying to shortchange the customer or by taking their frustrations out on the supplier. You have to remember that returns are a part of the business and in the end, they are inevitable. You should prepare for them by outlining clear rules on how they ought to be handled and by sticking to those rules even if things get frustrating.

Relying Too Much on One Supplier

Many dropshippers make the mistake of counting too much on a single supplier. This leaves them unprepared in case anything unexpected happens. You should always have several backup suppliers for every product in your store. If something happens, say your supplier runs out of stock or hikes up his prices, you can count on your backups to fill your orders. If you are in a situation where your business could live or die depending on the actions of a single supplier, then you are not managing your risks properly.

Failing to Test Several Products

You may have a niche in mind when you start your business, and you may select great products that bring in a decent profit, but that shouldn't be the end of it, you should keep testing new products to see if you can make money off of them. If you are inflexible about the products that you carry in your store, you could wake up one day to find that there is a universal shortage of your best-selling product, so it's good to have backup products. By testing several products, you can identify those that may come in handy when you want to scale your business.

Focusing on Price Competition

Many first-time dropshippers make the mistake of thinking that they can beat out the competition by setting their prices lower than everyone else. While it's true that customers like bargains and low prices, there are other more sustainable ways to make your store outshine from the competition. If you start a price war, you will be digging your own grave. Whenever businesses start undercutting each other, it's the ones that have few resources that end up losing. You cannot undercut dominant online retailers because they are always willing to match the lowest price, so you have to be unique by offering great service with a personal touch.

Selling Products That Violate Trademark or Copyright Laws

Just because a supplier has a product available in his inventory doesn't mean that it is entirely legal. There are many cases where suppliers stock knockoff products that are often imported from Asia. You may also see clothes or accessories with nice logos from popular Western franchises, and decide to sell them in your store. You should be extremely careful in these situations because some of those products may violate the legal rights of other businesses, and you could get sued by the companies that own the trademarks, copyrights, or other intellectual properties that were used to make those products.

16

16 [16] https://www.intelligencenode.com/blog/8-common-dropshipping-mistakes-avoid/

Conclusion

Thanks for making it through to the finish line of "The Next Level Dropshipping Guide: How to Elevate your Income and Create a Lucrative Long-term Business from Anywhere in the world with Facebook advertising, Shopify, And Fulfillment Centers." Let's hope it was enlightening and able to provide you with all of the tools you must have to reach your goals and dreams whatever they may be.

The next step is to use the steps that we talked about in this guidebook to help you get started with your own dropshipping business today. There are many distinguished ways to make money in our modern world. Some need a lot of effort and time though, and a good number of them are not going to offer you with a reasonable amount of money for the time and effort that you put into it at the beginning.

But when you get started with dropshipping, you will find that things can be different. You will truly run your own business without having to put a pile of money down and without having to hold inventory. A dropshipping business can easily have hundreds of products, and you never have to touch a single one in the process. And with this form of business, it is upon you to decide how big or small your business is at any given time.

This guidebook takes some time to dig in the dropshipping process and what it entails. We looked at the basics of dropshipping as well as some of its advantages and disadvantages to getting started with it. We then highlighted some basics of getting your own business up and running, how to pick out a good supplier and good products, and how to provide good customer service each and every time.

From there, we moved on to some of the different platforms that you can use to help make that business grow. We looked at Shopify, Amazon, eBay, and even using your own personal website, and the reasons that you would choose to work with each one.

To finish off, we spent some time talking about how you can use social media to enhance your business and spread the word, how Facebook marketing can help you to see more with your business. There are a lot of channels that you can use to promote and work on your own business, and this guidebook has covered those areas on how you can use all of them together to maximize profits for your business.

There may be a lot of different online businesses out there, but a good number of them are going to take a lot of time and cost a lot of money and inventory just to get your foot in the door. Dropshipping is different. It is available for anyone who is looking forward to starting off with their personal entrepreneurship process but who intends to minimize the risk level that they are dealing with for their own online business. The moment you are ready to start off in dropshipping, make sure to check out this guidebook to direct you.

Bibliography

Youderian, A., & Hayes, M. What is Dropshipping | How does Drop shipping work?. Retrieved from https://www.shopify.com/guides/dropshipping/understanding-dropshipping

Chou, S. Dropshipping - Does It Really Work And Can You Make Money? - MyWifeQuitHerJob.com. Retrieved from https://mywifequitherjob.com/why-dropshipping-isnt-as-easy-and-simple-as-you-think/

Gilmore, N. (2015). 7 Business Advantages of Drop Shipping - Multichannel Merchant. Retrieved from https://multichannelmerchant.com/blog/7-business-advantages-drop-shipping/

What Are the Disadvantages of Drop Shipping?. (2017). Retrieved from https://www.apsfulfillment.com/shipping-fulfillment/what-are-the-disadvantages-of-drop-shipping/

Kraly, A. Tips For Choosing The Best and Most Profitable eCommerce Niches. Retrieved from https://www.dropshiplifestyle.com/profitable-niche-selection-explained/

Ferreira, N. (2019). How to Write Epic Product Descriptions

That Sell - Oberlo. Retrieved from
https://www.oberlo.com/blog/write-epic-product-descriptions

How to List Products on Amazon: Complete Guide for FBA
Sellers - AMZFinder. (2018). Retrieved from
https://www.amzfinder.com/blog/list-products-amazon-
complete-guide-fba-sellers/

De Jesus, L. Make Your Drop Shipping Business Stand Out
With Visual Branding. Retrieved from
https://www.dropshiplifestyle.com/make-drop-shipping-
business-stand-visual-branding/

Defranco, D. (2018). Retrieved from
https://www.quora.com/How-do-I-market-my-dropshipping-
business

Kumar, B. (2017). How to Start Your Own Brand From Scratch
in 7 Steps — Branding. Retrieved from
https://www.shopify.com/blog/how-to-build-a-brand

Tanir, B. (2018). Ecommerce Pricing Strategies: Is Your Price
Right?. Retrieved from https://www.oberlo.com/blog/pricing-
strategy-for-ecommerce

Ofiana, M. 15 Customer Service Best Practices For Your Drop
Shipping Business. Retrieved from
https://blog.dsmtool.com/customer-service-best-practices-
drop-shipping-business/

Drop Shipping Business: 8 Marketing Tips to double your sales. Retrieved from https://beeketing.com/blog/drop-shipping-business-marketing/

How To Successfully Market A Dropshipping Business Using Facebook Ads. Retrieved from https://www.woodropship.com/blog/successfully-market-dropshipping-business-using-facebook-ads/

Martins, N. (2018). How to Set Up Your Shopify Store Step by Step - Oberlo. Retrieved from https://www.oberlo.com/blog/how-to-set-up-your-shopify-store

8 Common Dropshipping Mistakes to Avoid. (2016). Retrieved from https://www.intelligencenode.com/blog/8-common-dropshipping-mistakes-avoid/

www.ingramcontent.com/pod-product-compliance
Lightning Source LLC
Chambersburg PA
CBHW050643190326
41458CB00008B/2399